PILED-HIGH
POTATOES

PILED-HIGH
POTATOES

DELICIOUS AND NUTRITIOUS WAYS TO ENJOY
THE HUMBLE BAKED POTATO

HANNAH MILES

RYLAND PETERS & SMALL
LONDON • NEW YORK

For John and Katie,
who brought sunshine into my life x

Senior designer Toni Kay
Editor Miriam Catley
Head of production
  Patricia Harrington
Art director Leslie Harrington
Editorial director Julia Charles
Publisher Cindy Richards
Photography & prop styling
  Steve Painter
Food stylist Lucy McKelvie
Indexer Vanessa Bird

First published in 2019 by
Ryland Peters & Small
20–21 Jockey's Fields, London
WC1R 4BW
and 341 E 116th St, New York NY 10029
www.rylandpeters.com

10 9 8 7 6 5 4 3 2 1

Text copyright ©Hannah Miles 2019
Design and photographs copyright
© Ryland Peters & Small 2019

ISBN: 978-1-78879-082-6

Printed in China

A CIP record for this book is available from the British Library. US Library of Congress Cataloging-in-Publication Data has been applied for.

Notes:
• Both British (Metric) and American (Imperial plus US cups) measurements are included in these recipes for your convenience, however it is important to work with one set of measurements only and not alternate between the two within a recipe.
• All spoon measurements are level unless otherwise specified. A teaspoon is 5 ml, a tablespoon is 15 ml.
• All eggs are medium (UK) or large (US), unless specified as large, in which case US extra-large should be used. Uncooked or partially cooked eggs should not be served to the very old, frail, young children, pregnant women or those with compromised immune systems.
• Ovens should be preheated to the specified temperatures. We recommend using an oven thermometer. If using a fan-assisted oven, adjust temperatures according to the manufacturer's instructions.

CONTENTS

INTRODUCTION

The humble potato can be cooked in so many different ways, but I have to say my favourite of all is a jacket. Whether baked in the oven with crispy skins laden with butter, or soft and fluffy from the microwave, a jacket has to be one of the easiest meals to prepare. I am not about to start telling you that every time you make a jacket you need a long and complicated recipe – there are many instant toppings which need no cooking and some quick and easy suggestions are featured on the following pages. The beauty of a jacket potato is that with any of these simple toppings you have a delicious instant supper in no time at all.

However, the true potential of a potato is limitless. There really are very few savoury dishes that can't be tweaked to serve on top of a potato – after all, potatoes are often served as an accompaniment to many dishes, so why not use the potato as a base of the dish itself. This book is divided into Classics, Fish & Seafood, Veggie, Meat Feasts and Global potatoes and then for the more creative of you, the final chapter, Baked & Beyond, contains baked potatoes, but not as you know them, with a few clever twists to tantalize your taste buds.

In the Classics chapter are all my favourites – 4 cheese melt, homemade BBQ baked beans and Coronation chicken. There is also spicy buffalo chicken and for a double carb feast why not try a mac & jac. I love to serve fish on top of jacket potatoes and there are many delicious recipes in the Fish & Seafood chapter – a simple prawn marie rose, a spicy tuna melt, salmon and avocado and mackerel and horseradish. Jacket potatoes are a great base for any vegetarian or vegan dish and the Veggie chapter contains a spiced dhal or sweet grilled leeks with roasted pepper Romesco.

The Meat Feasts chapter does exactly what it says on the tin – lots of hearty meat dishes, such as steak and cheese, pepperoni pizza, goulash and the American classic sloppy Joe. These are my 'go-to' easy supper dishes when I have friends over.

Inspired by travels around the world, the Global jackets are topped with Cuban pork, pastrami and sauerkraut for a classic New York reuben, Chinese beef in black bean sauce, Indonesian satay chicken and Danish cucumber and salmon. For the adventurous amongst you, there is even the Scottish delicacy of haggis and whisky sauce. If you want to spice up your jackets, the Baked & Beyond chapter contains chicken and leek potato pies topped with puff pastry, giant hasselback potatoes, loaded skins, a lasagne inspired potato and even a cheese potato soufflé served in a crispy jacket skin. So, what are you waiting for – get your spuds in the oven and serve them any which way you please.

POTATO VARIETIES

There are thousands of species of potato available all around the world with over 80 commercial varieties available in the UK alone. It is one of the most staple of our food substances and popular worldwide. So the question is, which is the best potato to use to make the perfect jacket?

Potatoes can be categorized into groups based on their skin type and characteristics – the key groups being brown potatoes (russet), red potatoes, white potatoes, yellow/Yukon potatoes and purple potatoes. Potatoes vary by waxiness – baking potatoes need to be floury or mealy with a higher starch content, and some varieties of these are set out below.

Usually farmers' markets and supermarkets will help you a great deal with selecting the best potato for baking as they are sold in packs labelled 'baking potatoes'. The shops will use their experience and expertise to offer the best selection and so those sold as baking potatoes are always a safe bet for a crisp skin and fluffy internal texture. Look for good, large round potatoes without any blemishes on them.

For those of you interested in trying different types of potato, the varieties which make the best jackets are those that take on a fluffy texture when baked with a high starch content, classing them as 'floury'. Generally, these are larger potatoes so make for a good meal when baked. Some examples are Maris Piper, Russet, Desiree and King Edwards which are all great for jacket potatoes. You can also bake mini jackets and sweet potatoes as an alternative and details of these follows.

Maris Piper Potatoes are probably the most common potato, certainly in the UK, and are available countrywide in supermarkets. They have a firm and fluffy texture and are great for baking and will have a good crisp skin.

Russet Potatoes (also known as Idaho potatoes) are large potatoes, generally with very few eyes and which have a dry and fluffy texture.

Desiree Potatoes have a red skin and golden yellow flesh and a firm texture which makes them suitable for all types of uses, including baking.

King Edward are one of the oldest variety of potatoes. They are still very popular today and are widely available in supermarkets. These are large sized potatoes, so they are great for making substantial jacket potato meal.

New Potatoes/Charlotte Potatoes Although not traditionally classed as jacket potatoes, large new potatoes and Charlotte potatoes can be baked to make mini jacket potato canapés. Bake them in a moderate oven at 180°C (350°F) Gas 4 for about 30–40 minutes until they are soft when you insert a knife in the middle.

Blue/Purple Potatoes – these potatoes are available occasionally in supermarkets and specialized delis/farmers' markets and are a culinary treat – more for their unusual colour than anything else. Although they can be baked, they are generally small in size and therefore are not really suitable for a large jacket potato meal, however, they would make a good canapé baked and topped with soured/sour cream and chives.

Sweet Potatoes I have to say that as much as I enjoy a traditional jacket potato, I really love sweet potatoes. They have a wonderful flavour and colour and will go well with most of the toppings in this book so can be switched in as you see fit. They can be baked in the oven in about the same time as a regular potato but their skins will not become crisp like a traditional jacket due to moisture in the potato. There are different types of sweet potatoes some with vibrant orange flesh and some with a paler yellow flesh. All of them are suitable for baking and can be prepared in the same way as a traditional white potato. The cooking time will vary depending on the size of the sweet potato. They are also suitable for microwave cooking making sure that you prick the skin before cooking.

COOKING POTATOES

The good thing about jacket potatoes is that there are many ways to cook them. The actual cooking time needed will vary from potato to potato given that they are all different sizes. To test if the potato is cooked, insert a sharp knife and if the potato feels soft inside with no resistance to the knife, it is done. If you still feel some resistance, cook for a little while longer.

Oven Baked Preheat the oven to 200°C (400°F) Gas 6. Prick the skin of your potato and rub with a little salt. Place in the oven for about 1 hour, depending on the size of your potato. Test if the potato is cooked following the method in the introduction above. You can also use a baked potato spike for oven baking. The metal spike inserted into the centre of the potato means that it cooks quicker and will reduce the cooking time above.

Microwave Preparing a jacket in the microwave is the quickest way of cooking a jacket potato. Prick the skin with a fork and rub with a little salt. Microwave on full power for about 8 minutes and then test if the potato is cooked following the method in the introduction above.

BBQ or Open Flame Rub the potato skin with a little olive oil and season with salt. Prick the skin with a fork. Wrap the potato in a good layer of foil (or a double layer of foil if you are cooking in an open fire). Place the potatoes on the BBQ or into the fire and cook for about 1 hour. Test using the method in the introduction above.

Steam Bake Method It is said that partially cooking your potatoes by steam before baking locks in moisture. In order to do this, place the potatoes in a steamer basket on the hob/stovetop and steam for 20 minutes. Preheat the oven to 200°C (400°F) Gas 6. Place the potatoes in the preheated oven for a further 40 minutes until the skins are crisp.

Slow Cooker Slow cookers are ideal for cooking potatoes as you can put them on in the morning and leave them to cook slowly throughout the day, for perfectly fluffy potatoes when you have finished work. To do this, wrap the potatoes in foil and place in the bottom of your slow cooker. There are conflicting opinions on whether you should add a small cup of water to give extra steam or whether to add no water at all. In all honesty, both methods work well so it really is a matter of personal preference. Cook the potatoes for about 8–10 hours. Although the potatoes will not have crispy skins, cooking with this method they do taken on a slightly caramelized flavour, which I am rather partial to.

TO OIL OR NOT TO OIL? – THAT IS THE QUESTION
There is some debate about whether it is best to rub the skins of your potatoes with oil before baking them. Those that favour this say that it leads to a crispier skin. There are even some who advocate rubbing potato skins with duck fat or basting the skin regularly whilst cooking. It really is a matter of personal preference, but I do find that potato skins crisp well enough with no fat at all.

Potato Skin Rubs One of the benefits of giving an oil rub is that you can add spices and herbs to the oil which will add extra flavour to your potato. The best way to do this is to prick the potato all over and then place a tablespoon of oil into a clean sealable bag. I prefer to use olive oil or rapeseed oil, but any flavourless oil will work. Add your spices or herbs to the oil and then place your potato inside the bag and seal it. Rub the potato well and then remove it from the bag and place on your baking sheet.

Try adding the following to your oil:

1 teaspoon oregano or dried mixed herbs
1 teaspoon curry powder or garam masala
salt and freshly ground black pepper
2 teaspoons pesto
1 teaspoon harissa paste

FLAVOURED BUTTERS

One of the simplest ways to enjoy a baked potato is with butter and seasoned with salt and pepper. That said, for not much more effort you can make delicious flavoured butters that can add extra pep to your potato. The butters, once prepared, can be stored in greaseproof paper rolls in the freezer, where they will keep for up to a month. When you want to eat, you can just cut a slice of frozen butter in the flavour of your choice. You can add any flavourings and seasonings to butter. Some of my favourites are below:

Chilli Lime Butter Mix 100 g/½ cup of softened butter with the grated zest of 1 lime and ½ a red chilli/chile, deseeded and finely chopped. Season with salt and pepper. Wrap tightly into a log shape in greaseproof paper and store in the freezer for up to 1 month.

Lemon Caper Butter Mix 100 g/½ cup of softened butter with the grated zest of 1 lemon. Finely chop 1 tablespoon of capers (I prefer to use baby capers) and mix into the butter with 1 tablespoon of chopped parsley. Season with salt and pepper. Wrap tightly into a log shape in greaseproof paper and store in the freezer for up to 1 month.

Pesto Butter Mix 100 g/½ cup of softened butter with 1 tablespoon of pesto. Season with pepper. Wrap tightly into a log shape in greaseproof paper and store in the freezer for up to 1 month.

Walnut and Blue Cheese Finely chop 6 walnut halves and 50 g/¼ cup of blue cheese. Mix the walnuts and cheese into 100 g/½ cup of softened butter. Season with salt and pepper. Wrap tightly into a log shape in greaseproof paper and store in the freezer for up to 1 month.

Gentleman's Anchovy Butter Mix 100 g/½ cup of softened butter with the grated zest of 1 lemon, 6 anchovies preserved in oil, very finely chopped, 1 garlic clove crushed to a paste and 1 tablespoon of freshly chopped parsley. Season with salt and pepper. Wrap tightly into a log shape in greaseproof paper and store in the freezer for up to 1 month.

Harissa and Lemon Butter Mix 100 g/½ cup of softened butter with 2 heaped teaspoons of rose harissa paste and the grated zest of 1 lemon. Stir in 1 tablespoon of freshly chopped coriander/cilantro. Season with salt and pepper. Wrap tightly into a log shape in greaseproof paper and store in the freezer for up to 1 month.

Indian Spiced Butter Mix 100 g/½ cup of softened butter with 1 heaped tablespoon of mango chutney and 1 teaspoon of curry paste, whisking so that everything is well mixed. Season with salt and pepper. Wrap tightly into a log shape in greaseproof paper and store in the freezer for up to 1 month.

Herby Butter Finely chop 2 tablespoons of fresh herbs such as parsley, mint or chives. Mix into 100 g/½ cup of softened butter, season with salt and pepper. Wrap tightly into a log shape in greaseproof paper and store in the freezer for up to 1 month.

Garlic Butter Peel and crush 1–2 garlic cloves. Crush the garlic to a paste on a chopping board with some coarse sea salt using the back of a knife until you have a garlic purée. Stir into 100 g/½ cup of softened butter with 1 tablespoon of freshly chopped parsley and season with salt and pepper. Wrap tightly into a log shape in greaseproof paper and store in the freezer for up to 1 month.

Tomato Butter Finely chop 5–6 sundried tomatoes. Place in a bowl with 100 g/½ cup of softened butter and 1 tablespoon of sundried tomato purée. Mix everything together and season with salt and pepper. Wrap tightly into a log shape in greaseproof paper and store in the freezer for up to 1 month.

NO TIME TO COOK INSTANT JACKET RECIPES

The good thing about jacket potatoes is that if you are short of time there are a huge number of instant toppings for your potato with store-bought ingredients that only require assembly or minimum cooking. The possibility of simple suppers this way is endless.

HERE ARE SOME OF MY FAVOURITE IDEAS:

Cheese and beans Heat 1 x 400 g/14 oz. can of baked beans in tomato sauce. Grate some strong flavoured Cheddar cheese. Top your jacket with the beans and cheese adding butter, salt and pepper to your own taste. If you have time you can pimp the beans by adding some cooked bacon and a dash of Worcestershire sauce for a BBQ flavour.

Tuna mayo Drain a small can of tuna (100 g/3½ oz. drained weight) and break up with a fork in a bowl. Mix in a tablespoon or two of mayonnaise. How much depends on your own taste – I like quite a lot of mayonnaise in mine. Season with salt and pepper and place on top of an open baked potato. For more flavour ideas, you can add a tablespoon or two of finely chopped (bell) peppers or sweetcorn or a little sweet chilli/chili sauce.

Cottage cheese, ham and chives Empty a 300 g/10½ oz. tub of cottage cheese into a bowl. Cut about 2–3 slices of ham into thin strips and stir through the cottage cheese with a tablespoon of snipped chives. Season well with salt and pepper and place on top of your hot potato. You can replace the chives with some finely chopped pineapple for an alternative tasty treat.

Coleslaw To make your own coleslaw, finely grate or slice a carrot, some white cabbage and an onion and place in a bowl. Whisk together 2–3 tablespoons of mayonnaise, some salt and pepper, 1 teaspoon of wholegrain mustard and 2 teaspoons of cider vinegar and then pour over the vegetables and mix everything well together. Serve on top of a hot potato. If you don't have time to make your own coleslaw a tub of store bought coleslaw makes a great topping on top of a hot jacket potato, cut open and topped with a little butter. Supermarkets sometimes sell packs of chopped vegetables for coleslaw, which you can just mix with mayonnaise if you prefer. If you want a sprinkle topping on top of the coleslaw why not add some toasted pumpkin seeds or crisp bacon pieces?

Feta, edamame and chorizo Cut a whole cooking chorizo sausage into rings and place in a frying pan/ skillet over the heat until the chorizo starts to crisp. You do not need to add any oil to the pan as the chorizo will release oil as it cooks. Mix the hot chorizo with cubes of feta (about 100 g/3½ oz.) and some cooked edamame beans for a vibrant topping.

Soured/sour cream and chives Mix 300 g/1¾ cups soured/sour cream with 2 tablespoons of freshly snipped chives in a bowl and season with salt and pepper. Cut your potatoes open and top with the soured cream mixture. This will make enough to top two potatoes. As a simple canapés idea you can bake small new potatoes in the oven at 180°C (350°F) Gas 4 for about 30 minutes until soft, then cut a cross on top and top each with a little of the above mixture.

Anti-pasti Buy packs of salami and cured meats, preserved artichokes, olives and sun-dried tomatoes and offer these as a topping plate with slices of mozzarella cheese for your guests to select to top their potatoes.

Hummus and carrot Use a grater to coarsely grate a carrot and add a squeeze of lemon juice and some salt and pepper. Top your potatoes with a tub of hummus – there are many flavours of ready-made hummus in the supermarkets and any of these would work. Add the grated carrot on top of the hummus and season well with salt and pepper and serve straight away.

Greek beans and feta Use a jar of Greek giant beans in tomato sauce (approximately 250 g/9 oz.) and heat in a saucepan. Cut open your cooked potato and place the hot beans on top. Crumble over approximately 100 g/3½ oz. of feta cheese and sprinkle with freshly chopped parsley.

Deli-tubs If you are short of time, supermarkets sell a wide variety of prepared deli tubs with sandwich fillings – such as coronation chicken, egg mayo, couscous salad – any of these make quick and easy toppings for a potato.

Cheesy Grate any cheese you like and place on top of a potato with butter for a melted gooey topping.

Tomato and onion salad Finely slice 2 large ripe tomatoes. Peel and finely slice half an onion. Place the onion and tomatoes in a mixing bowl and drizzle

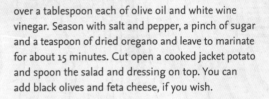

over a tablespoon each of olive oil and white wine vinegar. Season with salt and pepper, a pinch of sugar and a teaspoon of dried oregano and leave to marinate for about 15 minutes. Cut open a cooked jacket potato and spoon the salad and dressing on top. You can add black olives and feta cheese, if you wish.

Beef remoulade Grate 1 cored eating apple and 1 small onion on a coarse grater. Place in a mixing bowl and add in 2 tablespoons of natural/plain yogurt and 50 g/2 oz. of cream cheese and mix well together with a tablespoon of horseradish sauce. Season with salt and pepper. Cut open a cooked jacket potato and top with butter and some thin slices of roast beef and then add the apple salad on top.

Sweet marshmallow potatoes Bake a large sweet potato following the cooking instructions on page 11. Cut the potato open and scoop out the insides and place the potato flesh in a bowl and mash with a tablespoon of butter. Return the potato to the skins and sprinkle over 1 tablespoon of finely chopped pecan nuts. Cut about 10 marshmallows in half and place over the top of the potato. The number of marshmallows you will need depends on the size of your potatoes. Place under a hot grill/broiler for a few minutes until the marshmallows start to melt and caramelize. Take care that the marshmallows do not burn. Serve this twist on a Thanksgiving classic straight away.

CLASSICS

4 CHEESE MELT

A jacket topped with cheese is probably the most classic of all potato fillings. This is my pimped version with four types of cheese. You can use any cheese you like really, although I always like to finish with mozzarella on top, as this gives the potato a gooey cheesy topping.

2 large baking potatoes
75 g/scant 1 cup Cheddar cheese, grated
75 g/scant 1 cup red Leicester cheese, grated
2 tablespoons grated Parmesan cheese
1 tablespoon butter
1 ball mozzarella
salt and freshly ground black pepper

SERVES 2

Cook the potatoes following one of the methods on page 11.

Cut the potatoes open and scoop out the soft potato flesh into a bowl. Add all of the cheeses (other than the mozzarella) and the butter and season well with salt and pepper. Mash the potato so that it is light and fluffy and the cheese has melted. It is important to do this whilst the potatoes are hot otherwise the cheese will not melt. Spoon the cheese potato mixture back into the potato skins.

Preheat the grill/broiler to hot. Place the potato halves on a baking sheet lined with foil. Cut the mozzarella into thin slices and place some on top of each of the potatoes. Grill/broil under the hot grill/broiler until the mozzarella has melted and started to turn golden brown. Serve straight away.

DEVILLED EGG MAYO

Devilled eggs are a retro canapé and a favourite of my sister-in-law Amy. Traditionally, you remove the egg yolk and whisk it with mayo and paprika and then pipe it back into the cooked egg white to serve. In this potato version, I use the potato skin as a shell and then top with finely chopped egg white and pipe the devilled egg yolk into the centre to make a whole meal twist on the classic canapé. If you don't have a piping/pastry bag it is fine to just spoon the egg yolk mixture into the centre of the potato.

1 large baking potato
3 eggs
1 tablespoon mayonnaise
1 teaspoon Dijon mustard
½ teaspoon paprika,
    plus extra to serve
1 tablespoon butter
salt and freshly ground
    black pepper

*piping/pastry bag with
    large star nozzle/tip*

SERVES 1

Cook the potato following one of the methods on page 11. Place the eggs in a pan of cold water, bring to the boil, then simmer for 6 minutes. Immediately cool the eggs in cold water, then peel the shells. I find it best to do this by tapping the shell to crack it, then run the egg under cold water and peel the shell away. The running water makes this easy.

Cut the eggs in half and remove the yolks of the three eggs. Place the yolks in a mixing bowl with the mayonnaise, mustard and paprika and season with salt and pepper. Whisk the mixture together. To remove any lumps in the mixture, use a rubber spatula to rub the mixture against the side of the bowl. Once smooth, spoon the yellow egg mixture into the piping/pastry bag until you are ready to serve.

Whilst still hot, cut the potato in half and scoop out the middle. Place in a clean bowl with the butter, season with salt and pepper and mash until soft. Return the buttery mash to the potato skins.

Thinly slice two of the egg whites. You will not need all of the egg white so discard any you do not need (or finely chop and add to the mashed potato if you wish). Cover each potato with thin slices of egg white so that they are completely covered. Pipe a rosette of the egg yolk mixture into the centre of each potato half so that it looks similar to a devilled egg. Sprinkle with a little extra paprika, salt and pepper and serve straight away.

BBQ BAKED BEANS & PANCETTA

BBQ beans are the perfect campfire food – tangy with pancetta and Worcestershire sauce. If you are short of time, you can, of course, buy a can of ready-made BBQ beans but these honestly take so little time to prepare and taste so much nicer that it is really worth making if you can. If you are campfire cooking then simmering these in a pot over the fire whilst the potatoes cook wrapped in foil in the flames has to be just about the best supper you can serve whilst camping.

2 large baking potatoes
1 small onion,
    finely chopped
1 tablespoon olive oil
80 g/3 oz. pancetta cubes
250 ml/8½ oz. tomato
    passata/strained
    tomatoes
400 g/14 oz. can cannellini
    beans (drained weight
    246 g/approx. 9 oz.)
2 tablespoons
    Worcestershire sauce
2 tablespoons soy sauce
1 tablespoon maple sugar
    or brown sugar
butter or grated Cheddar
    cheese (optional)
salt and freshly ground
    black pepper

heavy-based saucepan

SERVES 2

Cook the potatoes following one of the methods on page 11.

In a heavy-based saucepan, cook the chopped onion in the olive oil until the onion is soft and starts to caramelise. Add the pancetta and fry until it is cooked through and starting to turn light golden brown. Add the passata/strained tomatoes to the pan and simmer. Drain the cannellini beans and rinse well in cold water. Add to the pan with the Worcestershire sauce, soy sauce and maple syrup or sugar, and simmer for about 15 minutes, stirring all the time until the sauce thickens. Season with salt and pepper.

Cut the potatoes open and top each with half of the beans. Add butter to the potato before topping with the beans if you wish or grated cheese for a more indulgent topping. Serve straight away.

HOT BUFFALO CHICKEN

I first tried hot buffalo chicken in Florida – it was one of those 'wow' dishes that on first eating you wonder how something can be so deliciously rich and naughty! The chicken filling is baked in the oven, so you can simply cook this at the same time as cooking the potatoes (once the potatoes are half-cooked) so that everything is ready together.

2 baking potatoes
200 g/scant 1 cup cream cheese
120 ml/½ cup ranch salad dressing
1–2 tablespoons red hot chilli/chili sauce (such as Franks)
200 g/2¼ cups Cheddar cheese, grated
200 g/7 oz. cooked chicken breast
salt and freshly ground black pepper
fresh snipped chives, to serve

ovenproof dish

SERVES 2

Preheat the oven to 180°C (350°F) Gas 4.

Place the baking potatoes in the preheated oven and cook for 30 minutes.

Whilst the potatoes are cooking, place the cream cheese, ranch dressing and hot sauce in a bowl and whisk together until smooth. Stir in the grated cheese. Remove any skin from the chicken breast and discard, then chop the chicken into small pieces. Stir the chopped chicken into the sauce. Season with black pepper and taste. You can add a little salt, if you wish, but I tend to find there is sufficient salt from the dressing and hot sauce. Spoon into an ovenproof dish.

Once the potatoes have cooked for 30 minutes, add the dish full of buffalo chicken to the oven and bake for 25–30 minutes until the top of the sauce starts to turn light golden brown. Remove from the oven, cut the potatoes in half and top with the hot chicken. Serve straight away, garnished with chives.

CORONATION CHICKEN

There are few more traditionally British fillings than Coronation Chicken, which was created for the banquet at the coronation of Queen Elizabeth II in 1953. This is a super quick and tasty supper to prepare – the sauce is ready in minutes.

1 baking potato
1 chicken breast, cooked and skin removed, cooled
1 tablespoon mayonnaise
1 tablespoon crème fraîche or soured/sour cream
1 tablespoon mango chutney or a handful of (dark) raisins
1 teaspoon curry powder
1 teaspoon black onion seeds
salt and freshly ground black pepper
freshly chopped coriander/cilantro or parsley, to garnish

SERVES 1

Cook the potato following one of the methods on page 11.

Chop the chicken breast into chunks and set aside.

In a bowl, whisk together the mayonnaise, crème fraîche or soured/sour cream, mango chutney, curry powder and black onion seeds. I like to use mango chutney with chunks so that you have pieces of fruit. Alternatively, you could add a handful of raisins for extra fruit, if you wish. Season with salt and pepper to your taste. Stir in the cold chicken making sure it is all coated in the sauce.

Cut the potato open and top with the Coronation Chicken. Garnish with a little coriander/cilantro or parsley, if you wish. Serve straight away.

MAC & JAC

This dish is the ultimate carb fest – pasta on potato – comfort food and perfect for winter evenings. The cheese sauce is the super quick kind that doesn't need a roux sauce and can be rustled up in just a few minutes.

2 baking potatoes
80 g/generous ½ cup
   macaroni

FOR THE QUICK
CHEESE SAUCE
60 g/generous ½ cup
   Cheddar cheese, grated
2 heaped tablespoons
   cream cheese
1 tablespoon butter
1 heaped teaspoon
   wholegrain mustard
salt and freshly ground
   black pepper

FOR THE BREADCRUMB
TOPPING
1 slice bread
olive oil

SERVES 2

Cook the potatoes following one of the methods on page 11.

Whilst the potatoes are cooking, cook the macaroni according to the packet instructions and then drain.

For the breadcrumb topping, blitz the bread in a blender to fine crumbs. Place the crumbs in a frying pan/skillet and drizzle with olive oil, then toast until golden brown. Set aside.

Place the grated Cheddar, cream cheese, butter and mustard in a saucepan and season with salt and pepper. Stir over a gentle heat until the cheese and butter have melted. Stir through the macaroni and heat until warmed through.

Cut the potatoes open and fill each with the macaroni cheese, then sprinkle with the toasted breadcrumbs. Serve straight away.

FISH & SEAFOOD

PRAWN MARIE ROSE

Prawn/shrimp cocktail was my Grandma's favourite dish. We have it every Christmas lunch as our starter to remember her. Prawn Mary Rose has to be one of the most popular jacket fillings and although good sauces are available to buy if you are short of time, nothing beats a proper homemade sauce. This is our family recipe. To make more portions, simply double or quadruple the ingredient quantities.

1 baking potato
100–150 g/3½–5½ oz.
   cooked, peeled
   prawns/shrimp

**FOR THE MARIE
ROSE SAUCE**
2 tablespoons mayonnaise
1 tablespoon tomato
   ketchup
1 tablespoon brandy
1 teaspoon horseradish
   sauce
1 teaspoon Worcestershire
   sauce
2 teaspoons freshly
   squeezed lemon juice
cayenne pepper or paprika,
   to taste
salt and freshly ground
   black pepper

TO SERVE
freshly snipped chives
lemon wedges

SERVES 1

Cook the potato following one of the methods on page 11.

For the Marie Rose sauce, whisk together the mayonnaise, ketchup, brandy, horseradish, Worcestershire sauce and lemon juice and season with a little cayenne pepper or paprika and salt and pepper. Taste and add a little more lemon juice if needed. Stir through the prawns/shrimp.

Cut open the potato and top with the prawns/shrimp and sauce. Sprinkle over some chives and season with a little more salt and pepper and a sprinkle of cayenne pepper or paprika for the classic orange dusting on a prawn cocktail. Serve straight away with lemon wedges to squeeze over.

MARYLAND CRAB

Maryland in America is famous for its crab and the many culinary delights that are made from them, often with a kick of chilli/chile. These crab loaded potatoes are similar to Welsh rarebit as the topping is made with egg and puffs up slightly when grilled, giving the potato a delicious fishy topping. They are great to serve as part of a buffet. Take care not to overfill the potatoes otherwise the topping may leak when cooking.

4 large baking potatoes
100 g/½ cup cream cheese
2 tablespoons soured/sour cream
1 tablespoon mayonnaise
1 tablespoon sweet chilli/chili sauce
1 teaspoon mustard
1 egg
100 g/3½ oz. white crab meat
2 tablespoons freshly grated Parmesan cheese
4 tablespoons panko breadcrumbs
lemon wedges, to serve
salt and freshly ground black pepper

SERVES 4

Cook the potatoes following one of the methods on page 11.

In a bowl, whisk together the cream cheese, soured/sour cream, mayonnaise, sweet chilli/chili sauce and mustard. Beat the egg and then whisk into the cream cheese mixture. Season with salt and pepper. Stir through the crab meat.

Cut the cooked potatoes in half. Using a spoon, remove about 1 cm/½ inch of cooked potato from each potato, leaving a little around the edges where the potato skin is. You want to make a cavity to fill with the crab mixture. Repeat with all the potatoes and place on a lined baking sheet that will fit under your grill/broiler. The removed potato is not needed for this recipe.

Preheat the grill/broiler to high.

Spoon the crab mixture into each of the potatoes. Sprinkle over the Parmesan and panko crumbs and season with a little more salt and pepper. Place carefully under the grill/broiler. Be careful not to tip the baking sheet so that the mixture does not spill out. Grill/broil for about 5 minutes until the top is golden brown and the crumbs are crisp. Serve straight away with lemon wedges to serve.

SALMON & AVOCADO
WITH SALMON CHIVE MOUSSE

Salmon and avocado is a winning combination and makes a great seafood jacket topping. The salmon mousse is easy to prepare in a blender but if you are short of time you could replace it with store-bought salmon pâté instead.

1 large baking potato
1 ripe avocado
lemon wedges, to serve
salt and freshly ground
   black pepper

FOR THE MOUSSE
100 g/3½ oz. smoked
   salmon
120 ml/½ cup double/
   heavy cream
freshly squeezed juice
   of 1 lemon
1 tablespoon finely chopped
   chives, plus extra
   to sprinkle

**FOR THE
LEMON BUTTER**
1 tablespoon butter,
   softened
½ teaspoon finely grated
   lemon zest (from the
   lemon above)

*piping/pastry bag and
   large star nozzle/tip*

SERVES 1

Cook the potato following one of the methods on page 11.

For the lemon butter, mix the butter with the lemon zest and season with salt and pepper and then wrap in greaseproof paper and store in the freezer until you are ready to serve.

To make the mousse, place half of the salmon in a blender with the double/heavy cream, half of the lemon juice and the chives and season with salt and pepper. Do not add too much salt as the salmon already tastes salty. Blitz on high power until the cream has thickened and you have a mousse-like consistency. Taste and add a little more salt and pepper or lemon juice, if you wish. Spoon the mousse into the piping/pastry bag when you are ready to serve.

Peel the avocado, remove the stone/pit and cut into slices. Toss the avocado in the remaining lemon juice to prevent it from discolouring. Cut the potato open and top with the lemon butter from the freezer. Place alternating slices of avocado and salmon on top of the potato. Pipe the salmon mousse over the top of the salmon and avocado and sprinkle with extra chives and a crack of black pepper. Serve straight away with lemon wedges to serve.

MACKEREL, BEETROOT & HORSERADISH

Whilst horseradish may be the traditional accompaniment to roast beef, it is also really delicious with smoked fish, particularly mackerel, as the sharpness of the sauce cuts through the oiliness of the fish. The fish is topped with thin strips of beetroot/beet, but if you prefer, you can top with beetroot/beet cubes instead if this is easier, or replace with some green salad leaves.

1 large baking potato
1 tablespoon olive oil
1–2 fresh mackerel fillets
   (depending on the size
   and how hungry you are)
salt and freshly ground
   black pepper

FOR THE
HORSERADISH CREAM
1 tablespoon horseradish
   cream
2 tablespoons crème fraîche

TO SERVE
butter for the potato (optional)
handful of peashoots
beetroot/beet strips
1 tablespoon chopped roasted
   hazelnuts
lemon wedges

SERVES 1

Cook the potato following one of the methods on page 11.

For the horseradish cream, stir the horseradish into the crème fraîche and season with salt and pepper. Store, covered, in the refrigerator until you are ready to serve.

Heat a griddle or frying pan/skillet and add the oil. Season the mackerel fillets and add to the pan and cook for 1–2 minutes on each side until the flesh is lightly golden brown. Once cooked, remove from the pan. Although you can eat the skin of the fish, if you prefer, you can remove it now peeling it away from the fish.

When you are ready to serve, cut the potato open and top with some butter, if using. Add the mackerel fillets and the horseradish cream. Top with the pea shoots, beetroot/beet and roasted hazelnuts and season with salt and pepper. Serve straight away with lemon wedges to squeeze over the fish.

TUNA MEXICANA MELT

This potato topping is a combination of two popular tuna dishes – tuna melt and tuna Mexicana. You can add any vegetables you like to the tuna mixture – I like avocado, (bell) peppers and corn but you can add kidney beans and chopped spring onions/scallions if you prefer. For the melted topping, I used Mexican flavour pepper Cheddar but you can replace with any melting cheese (such as mozzarella or regular Cheddar) of your choice.

1 large baking potato
1 tablespoon butter
salt and freshly ground
 black pepper

FOR THE FILLING
160 g/5½ oz. canned tuna,
 in water
2 tablespoons mayonnaise
1 tablespoon finely chopped
 (bell) pepper
1 tablespoon finely chopped
 white onion
1 tablespoon canned
 sweetcorn
½ teaspoon paprika
1 avocado, peeled, stoned/
 pitted and chopped into
 chunks
juice of 1 lime
70 g/scant cup Mexican
 pepper Cheddar
salt and freshly ground
 black pepper

SERVES 1

Cook the potato following one of the methods on page 11.

Whilst the potato is cooking, drain the tuna and place in a mixing bowl. Add the mayonnaise, chopped (bell) pepper, onion and sweetcorn. Season with the paprika and salt and pepper and stir well. Toss the avocado chunks in the lime juice and stir through gently. Store in the refrigerator until you are ready to serve.

When the potato is cooked, cut it in half and scoop out the potato flesh. Place in a large bowl and mash with the butter, then season with salt and pepper. Spoon the mashed potato back into the potato skins and place on a baking sheet which will fit under your grill/broiler. Preheat the grill/broiler to high.

Divide the tuna mixture between the two potato halves, spreading out so that it is even. Grate the pepper cheese and sprinkle over the two potato halves. Place under the hot grill/broiler for about 5 minutes until the cheese has melted and started to bubble. Serve straight away.

SALAD NICOISE

Salad Niçoise originated from the French town of Nice. It is a fresh and crisp tuna salad, rich with eggs and new potatoes and tangy from anchovies and capers. This recipe replaces the traditional new potatoes with a jacket potato to make this into a more substantial meal – perfect for summer suppers.

2 large baking potatoes
approx. 20 green beans,
    trimmed
1 egg
1 tuna steak
a little olive oil
6 cherry tomatoes
1 Little Gem/Bibb lettuce
2 tablespoons pitted
    black olives, halved
12 anchovies
butter, to serve
salt and freshly ground
    black pepper

FOR THE
CAPER DRESSING
1 teaspoon Dijon mustard
freshly squeezed juice
    of 1 lemon
2 tablespoons olive oil
2 teaspoons baby capers

SERVES 2

Cook the potatoes following one of the methods on page 11.

Whilst the potatoes are cooking, prepare the caper dressing. In a small bowl, whisk together the mustard, lemon juice and olive oil until emulsified. Whisk in the capers and set aside. If you cannot get small capers, you can use large capers and chop them finely. Store the dressing in the refrigerator until you are ready to serve.

In a saucepan of salted water, simmer the green beans for about 3–5 minutes until they are cooked. Drain and immediately blanch in cold water until they are chilled.

Boil the egg in a small pan of water, adding it to the pan when the water is boiling and simmer for 7 minutes for a medium soft-boiled egg. Drain and run under cold water and then peel off the shell. Cut the egg into quarters.

Heat a griddle pan until hot. Rub the tuna steak with a little olive oil and season with salt and pepper. Griddle for 1–2 minutes on each side, depending on how rare you like your tuna. Remove from the pan, cut into slices and leave to cool.

Cut the tomatoes in half and coarsely chop the lettuce. Place the tomatoes and lettuce in a bowl with the green beans, olives and anchovies. Spoon over the dressing and fold through.

When you are ready to serve, cut the potatoes open and top with butter. Divide the salad between the two potatoes and then add the tuna slices and egg quarters to each. Season with salt and pepper and serve straight away.

CREOLE SHRIMP
WITH TORTILLA CHIPS

Creole is a hot and spicy sauce traditionally made with (bell) pepper, tomatoes and hot sauce. It is a great combination with seafood. Although it's fiery, the taste is amazing and I like to serve it with crunchy tortilla chips to give extra texture to the dish.

2 large baking potatoes
1 red onion, chopped
1 stick celery, finely chopped
1 green (bell) pepper, deseeded and cut into thin strips
1 tablespoon olive oil
400 g/14 oz. can chopped tomatoes
2 tablespoons tomato purée/paste
125 ml/½ cup white wine
1 tablespoon hot sauce (such as Franks)
½ teaspoon cayenne pepper
150 g/5½ oz. cooked, peeled prawns/shrimp
2 tablespoons butter (optional)
a handful of tortilla chips
salt and freshly ground black pepper

SERVES 2

Cook the potatoes following one of the methods on page 11.

Place the onion, celery and (bell) pepper in a frying pan/skillet with the oil and cook for about 5 minutes until all are softened.

Add the tomatoes, tomato purée/paste and white wine to the pan and simmer for about 10 minutes until the sauce has thickened. Add the hot sauce to your taste. I usually add a tablespoon as I like it spicy, but reduce this a little, if you prefer. Add the cayenne pepper and taste for seasoning adding salt and pepper as needed.

When you are ready to serve, stir the cooked prawns/ shrimp into the sauce and heat through for a few minutes. If you prefer, you can use raw prawns/shrimp and cook them in the sauce for about 3–5 minutes until they turn pink.

To serve, cut the potatoes open and place on two plates. If you wish, you can scoop out the potato, mash with butter and then return to the skins. Top the potatoes with the prawns/shrimp and tomato sauce and place a few tortilla chips on top or alongside to serve. Serve straight away.

VEGGIE

CARROT & HUMMUS

Nothing beats a good homemade hummus – it is such a quick and easy dip to prepare with a few ingredients thrown into a blender with a can of pre-cooked chickpeas. You can pimp the flavour of the hummus, if you wish – try adding preserved (bell) peppers or some sweet chilli/chili sauce.

2 baking potatoes

FOR THE HUMMUS
400 g/14 oz. can chickpeas, rinsed and drained
2 tablespoons olive oil, plus extra to drizzle
½ teaspoon paprika or cayenne pepper (sweet or hot to your preference), plus extra to sprinkle
freshly squeezed juice of 2 lemons and grated zest of 1
1 garlic clove, peeled and finely chopped
2 tablespoons tahini
salt and freshly ground black pepper

FOR THE CARROT SALAD
1–2 small carrots
freshly squeezed juice of 1 lemon
1 tablespoon sesame seeds
1 tablespoon (dark) raisins

SERVES 2

Bake the potatoes following the instructions on pages 11.

Preheat the oven to 180°C (350°F) Gas 4.

Place a large tablespoon of the chickpeas in a roasting pan with a little drizzle of olive oil, some salt and pepper, a sprinkle of paprika and the lemon zest and bake in the preheated oven for 5–10 minutes until the chickpeas start to turn golden. Watch carefully towards the end of cooking to ensure that they do not burn.

Whilst the chickpeas and potatoes are cooking, make the rest of the hummus. Place the remaining chickpeas in a blender with the remaining olive oil, the lemon juice, paprika or cayenne pepper, garlic and tahini and a tablespoon or two of water and blitz to a smooth purée, adding a little more water if the mixture is too stiff. If you prefer a coarser hummus, place only half of the chickpeas into the blender at the start and blitz everything together, then once blended, add the remaining chickpeas and pulse until slightly chopped. Season the hummus with salt and pepper and a little more lemon juice or cayenne pepper to your own personal taste. Place in a container in the fridge topped with a little olive oil until you are ready to serve.

To prepare the carrot salad, peel the carrots and remove the ends, then spiralize into curls. If you do not have a spiralizer, then coarsely grate. Place the prepared carrot in a bowl and drizzle with the lemon juice. Stir through the sesame seeds and raisins. To serve, cut the potatoes open and top each with a large spoonful of hummus. Any leftover hummus will store in the refrigerator for a few days. Top with the carrot salad and sprinkle over the roasted chickpeas for added texture. Serve straight away.

MISO TOFU & MUSHROOM

On a recent trip to Japan, I discovered the delights of miso. Whilst here in the UK miso is mainly known in miso soup, in Japan I enjoyed it in a variety of ways, such as a dip for crudités and a sauce for noodle dishes. Tofu is a good source of protein and has a fairly neutral flavour so is a great vessel for this delicious miso sauce.

2 large baking potatoes
200 g/7 oz. tofu
1 tablespoon cornflour/
   cornstarch
1 tablespoon olive oil
1 tablespoon butter,
   plus extra for serving
200 g/7 oz. mixed
   mushrooms, such as
   enoki, shiitake or button
1 tablespoon miso paste
3 tablespoons mirin
dash of soy sauce
2 spring onions/scallions,
   finely chopped
salt and freshly ground
   black pepper

SERVES 2

Cook the potatoes following the instructions on page 11.

Cut the tofu into cubes. Pat dry on paper towels to remove as much moisture from the tofu as possible. Season the cornflour/cornstarch with salt and pepper and place on a plate. Toss the tofu in the cornflour/cornstarch. Heat the olive oil in a frying pan/skillet, add the tofu and fry on each side until lightly golden brown. Remove from the pan and drain any excess oil on the tofu on paper towels.

Add the butter to the frying pan/skillet with the mushrooms and season with salt and pepper. Pan-fry until the mushrooms are soft. Add the miso paste, mirin and the cooked tofu to the pan and cook for a few minutes to warm through. Season with a dash of soy sauce and stir in the chopped spring onions/scallions.

Cut the jacket potatoes open and top each with some butter and half of the tofu mixture. Serve straight away.

GRILLED LEEKS & ROMESCO SAUCE

When grilled/broiled, leeks take on a sweetness which is delicious on top of a jacket potato. Romesco sauce is a classic Spanish sauce made of red peppers and almonds and is delicious served with roasted leeks.

2 baking potatoes
1 large leek or 2 small leeks
olive oil, for drizzling
salt and freshly ground
  black pepper

**FOR THE
ROMESCO SAUCE**
1 thick slice white bread
100 g/¾ cup whole
  blanched almonds
4 slices preserved flame
  roasted red (bell) peppers
  (such as Gaea)
1 garlic clove, peeled
  and finely chopped
2 tablespoons sherry
  vinegar
1 teaspoon paprika
2 tablespoons olive oil
1 tablespoon tomato
  purée/paste

SERVES 2

Cook the potatoes following the instructions on page 11.

Trim the leeks and cut into long thin strips, washing well so that they are completely clean. Pat dry. Lay the leeks on a sheet of foil on the grill/broiler tray and drizzle with a little olive oil. Season with salt and pepper and cook under a hot grill/broiler for about 10–15 minutes until the leeks are soft and have started to char a little. Watch closely towards the end of cooking so that they do not burn. The time needed will depend on the temperature of your grill/broiler.

Preheat the oven to 180°C (350°F) Gas 4.

Whilst the leeks are cooking, prepare the Romesco sauce. Place the slice of bread and almonds on a baking sheet and bake in the oven for 5 minutes, so that the bread is crisp and the nuts have started to release their oil and are lightly golden brown. Place the bread and almonds in a food processor or blender with the (bell) peppers, garlic, sherry vinegar, paprika, oil and tomato purée/paste and blitz to a smooth paste. Season with salt and pepper.

To serve, cut the potatoes open and place half of the leeks on each. Top with a generous spoonful of Romesco sauce and serve straight away. Any leftover Romesco can be stored in the refrigerator for up to 3 days, by placing it in a jar and covering the top with a little olive oil.

CHILLI EGGS & AVOCADO

One of my favourite brunch dishes is eggs and avocado topped with crème fraîche and coriander/cilantro. Served on top of a potato this becomes a hearty dish. As an alternative, you can replace the scrambled egg with a poached or fried egg instead, sprinkled with a little paprika. Use more eggs if you are hungry.

2 large baking potatoes
1 avocado
freshly squeezed juice
of 1 lemon
2 tablespoons butter
1 teaspoon deseeded,
chopped red chilli/chile,
plus extra to garnish
6 eggs
2 tablespoons milk
or cream
2 tablespoons crème fraîche
freshly chopped
coriander/cilantro
salt and freshly ground
black pepper

SERVES 2

Bake the potatoes following the instructions on page 11.

Cut the avocado in half and remove the stone/pit. Squeeze with lemon juice to prevent it from discolouring. Set aside whilst you cook the eggs.

Melt the butter in a large frying pan/skillet. Add the chilli/chile to the butter and cook for a few minutes until soft. Whisk the eggs with the milk or cream and season with salt and pepper. Pour into the foaming butter and cook, stirring all the time, until the eggs are cooked.

Cut the potatoes open and divide the eggs between the potatoes. Top each with half an avocado and a large spoonful of crème fraîche. Sprinkle with fresh coriander/cilantro and season with salt and pepper. Serve straight away.

CAULIFLOWER CHEESE

If you like cauliflower, then this is the dish for you! The cauliflower is used two ways in the dish – firstly creamed and mashed into the potato filling and secondly as a topping with a rich cheese sauce.

4 large baking potatoes
30 g/1 oz. panko
    breadcrumbs
1 tablespoon olive oil
1 head of cauliflower, leaves
    and stalk removed and
    chopped into florets
approx. 1 litre/4 cups milk
2 tablespoons butter

FOR THE CHEESE SAUCE
3 tablespoons butter
3 tablespoons plain/
    all-purpose flour
300 ml/1¼ cups of the
    reserved milk from
    above from cooking
    the cauliflower
180 g/scant 2 cups
    Cheddar cheese, grated
pinch of freshly grated
    nutmeg
salt and freshly ground
    black pepper

SERVES 4

Cook the potatoes following the instructions on page 11.

In a frying pan/skillet, fry the breadcrumbs in the oil until they are golden and toasted. Set aside until you are ready to serve.

Put the chopped cauliflower in a large saucepan and pour over enough milk to cover it. Heat the pan over a medium heat so that the milk becomes hot and then simmer for about 5–10 minutes until the cauliflower is soft. Drain the cauliflower through a sieve/strainer, reserving the warm milk. Keep the cauliflower warm.

For the cheese sauce, heat the butter in a saucepan over a gentle heat until melted, then add the flour and whisk to incorporate. Cook for a few minutes over the heat taking care that the flour mixture does not burn. Slowly whisk 300 ml/1¼ cups of the reserved cauliflower milk in a little at a time. Add the cheese to the white sauce and whisk over a gentle heat until the cheese has melted and the sauce has thickened. Season with salt and pepper and a little nutmeg. If there are any lumps in the sauce pass it through a fine mesh sieve. Keep warm until you are ready to serve. To prevent a skin from forming you can place a piece of clingfilm/plastic wrap directly onto the surface of the sauce.

Place a third of the cauliflower in a food processor with the 2 tablespoons of butter and 100 ml/⅓ cup of the remaining cauliflower milk and blitz to a smooth purée. Place in a bowl. Cut open the cooked potatoes and scoop out the soft potato inside. Mash the purée and potato together and season with salt and pepper. Spoon the cauliflower potato back into the potato skins. Place a potato on each serving plate and divide the remaining cauliflower between the plates. If your cauliflower was very large, you may not need all of it. Pour the cheese sauce over each potato and top with the toasted breadcrumbs. Season and serve.

WELSH RAREBIT

I know I am biased as I am half Welsh (thanks Dad), but this humble dish, originating from Wales, is hard to beat. It has its origins as long ago as the 15th century and used to be called 'Caws Pobi' – literally baked cheese. It is, in reality, just posh cheese on toast – but my, it is good! This is my potato version!

2 large baking potatoes
1 egg
100 g/generous 1 cup
 Cheddar cheese
1 heaped teaspoon
 wholegrain mustard
2 teaspoons Worcestershire
 sauce, plus extra for
 sprinkling after cooking
1 heaped tablespoon butter
salt and freshly ground
 black pepper

TO SERVE
green salad

SERVES 2

Bake the potatoes following the instructions on page 11.

Once the potatoes have almost finished cooking in the oven, prepare the rarebit topping. Beat the egg and grate the cheese, then mix the grated cheese into the egg with the mustard and Worcestershire sauce. Season with salt and pepper.

Preheat the grill/broiler to high. Cut each potato in half. Scoop out the soft potato into a bowl and mash with the butter, then season with salt and pepper. Spoon the potato back into the potato skins and place on a baking sheet.

Spoon a quarter of the rarebit mixture over each potato half and grill/broil under the hot grill/broiler for about 5 minutes, until the mixture has puffed up and the cheese has started to turn golden brown on top. Remove from the grill/broiler and serve straight away with a green salad to cut through the richness of the cheese. Top with a dash of extra Worcestershire sauce just before serving.

RATATOUILLE WITH GOAT'S CHEESE

The best thing about a ratatouille is that you can make a giant pan of it with minimal preparation. Ratatouille can be used in a wide variety of ways – such as tossed through pasta or served cold as a salad, but my favourite is to serve it piled high on a jacket. If you are not fond of goat's cheese, you can top with grated cheese or a natural yogurt with a little harissa stirred through instead.

2 baking potatoes
1 aubergine/eggplant
2 courgettes/zucchini
1 small onion
2 garlic cloves, peeled
1 pepper
4 tomatoes
60 ml/¼ cup white wine
2 tablespoons plus
    1 teaspoon olive oil
1 teaspoon dried oregano
1 teaspoon finely chopped
    rosemary
3 tablespoons freshly
    chopped basil, plus
    extra for serving
4 slices of round goat's
    cheese
1 teaspoon clear honey
salt and freshly ground
    black pepper
butter, to serve

SERVES 4

Bake the potatoes following the instructions on page 11.

Preheat the oven to 180°C (350°F) Gas 4.

Trim the top of the aubergine/eggplant and then cut the remainder into 3 cm/1¼ inch cubes. Trim the tops of the courgettes/zucchini and cut into discs. Peel the onion and cut into wedges. Finely chop the garlic. Deseed the (bell) pepper and cut into strips. Cut each of the tomatoes into quarters. Add all of the ingredients above into a roasting pan and pour over the wine and 2 tablespoons of the oil, season well with salt and pepper and add the oregano, rosemary and basil. Roast in the preheated oven for about 30 minutes (during the second half of the potatoes cooking) until the vegetables are all soft. Remove from the oven and stir through.

Preheate the grill/broiler to high. Place the slices of goat's cheese under a hot grill/broiler and drizzle with a little honey and the olive oil and season with salt and pepper. Grill/broil for a few minutes until the cheese starts to melt and caramelize.

To serve, cut the potatoes open and top with some butter and then a generous spoonful of ratatouille. Top each potato with a slice of goat's cheese and serve straight away with extra fresh basil.

ASPARAGUS & TARRAGON HOLLANDAISE

Fresh asparagus dipped in hollandaise is one of the nicest things to eat in the spring asparagus season. Making hollandaise is not as tricky as you may think. This hollandaise is flavoured with tarragon and I really love the slight aniseed hint this gives, but you can replace with a bay leaf, if you prefer.

2 large baking potatoes
16 asparagus spears

FOR THE HOLLANDAISE
1 tablespoon white wine
 vinegar
freshly squeezed juice
 of 1 lemon
1 teaspoon dried or freshly
 chopped tarragon
1 whole egg
2 egg yolks
190 g/generous ¾ cup
 butter
salt and freshly ground
 black pepper

SERVES 2

Bake the potatoes following the instructions on page 11.

For the hollandaise, simmer the vinegar and lemon juice in a saucepan with the tarragon for a few minutes to reduce the liquid. Strain to remove the tarragon and season the liquid with salt and pepper. Place the liquid in a food processor or blender with the egg and egg yolks and blend together. Melt the butter in a saucepan, cool slightly, and then, with the blade still running and the butter warm, pour into the egg mixture in a thin drizzle. Whisk until the mixture becomes slightly thick. Taste for seasoning and acidity, adding a little further lemon juice and salt and pepper if needed. Keep warm whilst you steam the asparagus.

Boil water in the pan below the steam basket. Once boiling, add the asparagus to the pan, cover with a lid and steam for about 5 minutes. The actual cooking time will depend on the thickness of your asparagus. It should still be bright green and a little crisp – there is nothing worse than soggy asparagus!

Cut the potatoes open and top each with half of the asparagus. Spoon over a generous portion of hollandaise and top with a little black pepper. Serve straight away.

ARTICHOKE & OLIVE ROCKET SALAD WITH PARSLEY CAPER DRESSING

I have always loved olives but when roasted they take on a whole new dimension. Baked here with artichokes, they form a fresh and delicious warm salad filling for a jacket potato. I love to add a tangy lemon and caper dressing to cut through the oil of the olives and artichokes.

2 baking potatoes
10 artichoke heart quarters, preserved in oil
about 20 olives (black or green), preserved in olive oil or marinated if you prefer
large handful of rocket/arugula

FOR THE CAPER PARSLEY DRESSING
grated zest and freshly squeezed juice of 1 lemon
1 tablespoon olive oil
2 teaspoons Dijon mustard
1 tablespoon freshly chopped parsley
2 teaspoons baby capers
salt and freshly ground black pepper

SERVES 2

Cook the potatoes following the instructions on page 11.

Preheat the oven to 180°C (350°F) Gas 4.

Place the artichokes and olives on a baking sheet and bake in the preheated oven for about 5–10 minutes. As they are marinated in oil, you do not need to add any further oil for cooking.

Whilst the olives are cooking, prepare the dressing by whisking together the lemon zest and juice, olive oil and mustard until emulsified. Whisk in the parsley and capers. If you can only get large capers rather than baby capers, roughly chop them with a sharp knife. Season the dressing with salt and pepper.

To serve, cut each potato open. Toss the rocket/arugula with the artichokes and olives (together with any roasting juices) and divide between the potatoes. Drizzle the dressing over the potatoes. Serve straight away.

GREEK SALAD WITH FETA

White buildings with blue doors, sunshine and windmills, ouzo and feta salad are to me the memories of Greece. Greek salad is packed full of flavour with fresh vegetables and sharp feta cheese with a heady fragrance of oregano. It makes a light and fresh summer topping for a baked potato. Pickling the onion in a little vinegar and sugar produces a bright pink colour and tastes divine.

2 baking potatoes
butter, to serve

FOR THE ONIONS
1 small red onion
2 tablespoons white wine
   vinegar
2 teaspoons white sugar

FOR THE SALAD
½ cucumber
2 large tomatoes
100 g/¾ cup feta cheese
75 g/¾ cup pitted
   black olives
2 tablespoons freshly
   chopped basil

FOR THE DRESSING
2 tablespoons olive oil
1 tablespoon cider vinegar
1 teaspoon dried oregano
1 teaspoon Dijon mustard
½ teaspoon white sugar
salt and freshly ground
   black pepper

SERVES 2

Cook the potatoes following the instructions on page 11.

Peel and halve the onion and cut into very thin slices. Place in a bowl and pour over the vinegar and sugar. Leave for about 30 minutes for the onion to soften. Stir occasionally to make sure that the sugar has dissolved.

To prepare the salad, trim the ends off the cucumber and peel away the green skin using a swivel vegetable peeler. Cut in half lengthways and remove the inner seeds using a teaspoon. Cut the cucumber into slices and place into a bowl.

Cut the tomatoes in half and remove all of the seeds with a spoon. Cut the tomatoes into pieces and place in the bowl. Cut the feta cheese into cubes and add to the salad with the olives and the basil. Drain the onion and discard the vinegar, then add the onions to the salad.

For the dressing, place all the ingredients in a bowl and whisk together. Taste and adjust the seasoning to your own preference. Pour the dressing over the salad and stir gently so that all of the salad is lightly coated in dressing. Cover and place in the fridge for about 20–30 minutes to chill. When you are ready to serve, cut open the potatoes, add butter and seasoning and top each with a large portion of the salad. Serve straight away.

AUBERGINE WITH HARISSA, CRÈME FRAÎCHE & TOASTED PINE NUTS

Aubergine/eggplant roasted with olive oil until crisp makes a fantastic potato topping. In this recipe, it's roasted with tomatoes, garlic and onion to give a Mediterranean flavour. Topped with crème fraîche and pine nuts and a drizzle of harissa, this makes a perfect lunch dish. I love to use rose harissa as it has a perfumed flavour. It is important to use a harissa which is oily so that it is easy to spoon over.

2 large baking potatoes
1 aubergine/eggplant
10 cherry tomatoes
½ small onion
1 garlic clove
½ large red chilli/chile, deseeded and finely chopped
2–3 tablespoons olive oil
2 tablespoons pine nuts
2 tablespoons crème fraîche
1 tablespoon harissa paste

SERVES 2

Cook the potatoes following the instructions on page 11.

Preheat the oven to 180°C (350°F) Gas 4.

Cut the top and bottom away from the aubergine/eggplant and cut into 3 cm/1¼ inch cubes. Cut the tomatoes in half. Peel and thinly slice the onion and garlic. Place the onion, garlic and chilli/chile in the bottom of a roasting pan, spreading out evenly and cover with the aubergine/eggplant. Drizzle with the olive oil so that all the aubergine/eggplant is coated in oil. Bake in the preheated oven for about 30–40 minutes until the aubergine/eggplant has started to crisp and the rest of the vegetables are soft. Check halfway through cooking and drizzle over a little more olive oil if needed.

Meanwhile, place the pine nuts in a dry frying pan/skillet and toast over a gentle heat until they start to turn golden brown. Stir all the time as they can burn easily.

When you are ready to serve, cut the potatoes open and place on serving plates. Stir the aubergine/eggplant mixture and divide between the potatoes. Top each with a large spoonful of crème fraîche and sprinkle over the toasted pine nuts. Drizzle with a little harissa for a spicy kick and serve straight away.

THREE BEAN VEGAN CHILLI
WITH CHARRED SWEETCORN & SALSA

4 large baking potatoes
1 corn on the cob/ear
 of corn, peeled
a little olive oil

FOR THE CHILLI
1 tablespoon olive oil
1 small onion,
 finely chopped
1 red chilli/chile, deseeded
 and finely chopped
2 garlic cloves, sliced
400 g/14 oz. can kidney
 beans in chilli/chili sauce
400 g/14 oz. can
 cannellini beans
300 g/10½ oz. can
 haricot beans
400 g/14 oz. can chopped
 tomatoes
70 g/2½ oz. tomato
 purée/paste
1 teaspoon paprika
salt and freshly ground
 black pepper

FOR THE SALSA
3 tomatoes
1 ripe avocado
2 spring onions/scallions,
 thinly sliced
freshly squeezed juice
 of 1 lime
1 tablespoon olive oil

SERVES 4

This vegan spicy bean chilli is served with charred sweetcorn and a fresh and zingy salsa. If you don't have time to char the sweetcorn you can just use a spoonful or two of canned sweetcorn in its place. This makes a large pan of chilli but it freezes well so if you do not need to feed four, freeze the left over chilli in individual portions.

Cook the potatoes following one of the methods on page 11.

Brush the corn on the cob with a little oil, place in a hot griddle pan and cook for about 15 minutes until the corn has started to char on all sides. Remove from the heat and let cool.

For the chilli, heat the olive oil in a pan and fry the onion, chilli/chile and garlic until the onion has softened and started to turn light golden brown. Add the kidney beans and sauce to the pan. Rinse the cannellini and haricot beans under cold water and then add them to the pan. Add the tomatoes, 250 ml/1 cup plus 1 tablespoon of water and the tomato purée /paste and season with salt, pepper and the paprika. Simmer for 30 minutes over a gentle heat until the sauce thickens.

To prepare the salsa, remove the seeds from the tomatoes and chop into small pieces. Remove the skin and stone from the avocado and chop into small pieces. Add the spring onions/scallions, lime juice and oil to the tomatoes and avocado and toss everything together then season. Cover and chill in the refrigerator until you are ready to serve.

Place the corn on a chopping board and with a sharp knife, cut the kernels off, in slices.

To serve, cut the potatoes open and top each with a portion of chilli. Top with the corn slices and salsa and serve.

MEAT FEASTS

STEAK & CHEESE

Steak and cheese combo not only makes a great sandwich but is a perfect topping for a potato. The steak is served on a bed of warm caramelized onion and (bell) pepper and with gooey cheese this makes a really filling and tasty supper.

2 baking potatoes

FOR THE CARAMELIZED ONION AND (BELL) PEPPERS
1 red (bell) pepper, deseeded
1 brown onion, finely sliced
1 tablespoon olive oil
1 teaspoon balsamic glaze
  or vinegar
1 teaspoon caster/
  granulated sugar

TO SERVE
1 sirloin steak
olive oil
4 slices Swiss cheese
salt and freshly ground
  black pepper

SERVES 2

Cook the potatoes following one of the methods on page 11.

To make the caramelized onion and (bell) pepper, finely slice the (bell) pepper and add to a frying pan/ skillet with the onion and olive oil and cook for about 5–8 minutes until the pepper is soft and the onion starts to caramelize. Once softened, add the balsamic glaze or vinegar and sugar to the pan and cook for a few minutes until caramelized. Set aside, but keep warm.

Heat a griddle pan until it is searingly hot. Rub the steak with a little olive oil and season with salt and lots of pepper. Place in the griddle pan and sear for 1–2 minutes on each side. Remove from the pan and leave to rest for a few minutes then cut into thin slices.

Cut the potatoes open and divide the onion and (bell) pepper mixture between them, cover each with two slices of cheese and top with the steak. Serve straight away.

STICKY SWEET CHILLI CHICKEN

This spicy chicken topping is so simple to prepare as it uses sweet chilli sauce instead of a marinade. It's readily available in supermarkets and Asian food shops. With hints of ginger, garlic and spring onion/scallion, take out your wok and this topping will be ready in no time.

2 large baking potatoes
1 small onion, finely chopped
2.5-cm/1-inch piece of ginger, peeled and finely chopped
1 garlic clove, finely chopped
1 tablespoon olive oil
2 chicken breasts, skinless
2 spring onions/scallions
8 broccoli florets, halved
2–3 tablespoons sweet chilli sauce
1 tablespoon clear honey
freshly squeezed juice of 1 lime
salt and freshly ground black pepper

SERVES 2

Cook the potatoes following one of the methods on page 11.

Place the onion, ginger and garlic in a wok with the oil and stir-fry until the onion is soft and translucent. Cut the chicken into cubes, add to the wok and stir-fry for about 8–10 minutes until the chicken is cooked through.

Chop the spring onions/scallions into pieces, add to the wok with the broccoli and stir-fry for a few minutes.

Add the sweet chilli/chili sauce, honey and lime juice to the wok and season well with salt and pepper.

Cut the potatoes open, divide the chicken mixture between the potatoes and serve straight away.

BACON, BRIE & CRANBERRY

Bacon, brie and cranberry is a popular sandwich filling, so why not serve it on top of a potato? This one is very quick and easy to make and needs minimum preparation so is a great supper to rustle up after work. You can use back bacon in place of the streaky bacon, if you prefer.

1 large baking potato
4 rashers/slices smoked
    streaky bacon
1 tablespoon butter
2 tablespoons cranberry
    sauce
75 g/2½ oz. ripe brie cheese
salt and freshly ground
    black pepper

SERVES 1

Cook the potato following one of the methods on page 11.

In a frying/skillet or griddle pan, cook the bacon for about 5 minutes until crisp and golden brown.

Cut the potato in half and scoop out the soft potato middle. Reserve the skins. Place the potato in a bowl and mash with the butter until soft, then season well with salt and pepper. Scoop the potato back into the skins and place in an ovenproof dish or baking sheet.

Preheat the grill/broiler to high.

Place two rashers/slices of bacon on each potato half and top with a spoonful of cranberry sauce. Cut the brie into slices and place on top of each potato half.

Place the potato halves under the grill/broiler for about 5 minutes until the brie has melted and is gooey. Serve straight away.

WINNER WINNER CHICKEN DINNER

4 large baking potatoes

FOR THE CHICKEN
3 tablespoons cream cheese
1 spring onion/scallion,
    trimmed and finely
    chopped
1 small whole fresh chicken
    (approx. 1–1.2 kg/35–44 oz.)
olive oil, to drizzle
salt and freshly ground
    black pepper

FOR THE STUFFING
1 tablespoon olive oil
1 carrot, peeled and
    finely chopped
1 onion, finely chopped
1 garlic clove, finely
    chopped
1 stick celery, finely chopped
4–5 slices bread, chopped
    into small cubes – sour
    dough works well
2 bay leaves
400 ml/1¾ cups good-
    quality chicken stock

FOR THE GRAVY
1 small onion, finely
    chopped
1 tablespoon olive oil
2 tablespoons butter
200 ml/1 cup Madeira
    or sweet sherry
600 ml/2½ cups chicken
    stock
2 tablespoons
    cornflour/cornstarch

SERVES 4

This is a meal in one with the chicken and stuffing served on top of a jacket.

Cook the potatoes following one of the methods on page 11.

Preheat the oven to 180°C (350°F) Gas 4.

To prepare the chicken, in a bowl, mix together the cream cheese and spring onion/scallion with a fork and season well. Slide your finger under the chicken skin carefully to create a pocket. Using your finger, spread the cream cheese mixture under the skin, spreading it out evenly by running your finger over the top of the skin once the cream cheese is inside. Place in a roasting pan, drizzle with a little olive oil and season. Roast for about 1¼ hours until golden brown. The chicken is cooked when the juices run clear when you insert a knife into the thickest part of the chicken.

For the stuffing, heat the olive oil in a large frying pan/skillet and sauté the carrot, onion, garlic and celery for about 15 minutes over a gentle heat until they are all soft and the onion is translucent. Spoon into a separate roasting pan and add the bread and bay leaves. Stir, season and pour over the stock. Place in the oven and cook for 30–40 minutes stirring occasionally. The stuffing is done when the stock has evaporated and the bread is crispy.

For the gravy, place the onion in a saucepan with the olive oil and half of the butter, season and simmer over a gentle heat until the onion is very soft and starting to caramelize. Add the Madeira or sherry to the pan and simmer until the liquid has reduced to a quarter. When the liquid is thick and syrupy add the stock to the pan and continue to simmer until the liquid is reduced by a third. In a small bowl, rub the remaining butter into the cornflour with your fingertips to make a roux. To thicken the gravy, add the roux to the pan, a little at a time whisking all the time. You may not need all of the roux. When thickened, pass the gravy through a fine mesh sieve to remove the onion and keep warm until you are ready to eat. Top each potato with some of the stuffing and chicken slices and serve with gravy.

SLOPPY JOE

Sloppy Joe is an American classic. Minced/ground beef cooked with tomatoes and a sweet and sour flavour from sugar and Worcestershire sauce. This is traditionally served in a burger bun but works well on a potato. This is my USA tribute served with caramelized (bell) peppers!

4 large baking potatoes
4 slices processed cheese
  (optional)

**FOR THE CARAMELIZED
(BELL) PEPPERS**
3 (bell) peppers, deseeded
  and sliced
1 tablespoon olive oil
2 teaspoons balsamic glaze
  or vinegar
1 teaspoon soft brown sugar

**FOR THE MINCED/
GROUND BEEF**
1 onion, finely chopped
1 tablespoon olive oil
400 g/14 oz. ground/
  mince beef
500 ml/17 oz. passata/
  strained tomatoes
70 g/2½ oz. tomato
  purée/paste
2 tablespoons brown sugar
1–2 tablespoons
  Worcestershire sauce
2 teaspoons wholegrain
  mustard
salt and freshly ground
  black pepper

SERVES 4

Cook the potatoes following one of the methods on page 11.

For the caramelized (bell) peppers, place the peppers in a frying pan/skillet with the oil and cook until they are soft which will take about 5 minutes. Add the balsamic glaze or vinegar and sugar to the pan and cook for a few more minutes until the (bell) peppers start to caramelize. Remove from the heat and reheat just before serving (or keep warm).

For the minced/ground beef, place the chopped onion in a large casserole with the oil and cook for 3–5 minutes until the onion is softened. Add the beef to the pan and cook until all of the beef has turned brown. Add the passata/strained tomatoes, tomato purée/paste, brown sugar, Worcestershire sauce and mustard and season well with salt and pepper. Simmer for about 25–30 minutes, stirring regularly so that it does not stick, until the sauce has thickened.

To serve, cut the potatoes open and top with the Sloppy Joe and (bell) peppers, adding in a slice of processed cheese between the meat and (bell) peppers if you wish. Serve immediately. Any leftover beef can be frozen in individual portions for another day and will store for up to 1 month.

PIZZA POTATOES

I don't know anyone who doesn't love a good pizza –
especially children. These potatoes make a great alternative
for kids' parties and you can top with any classic pizza
toppings you like. You could even have people assemble
their own and then make them to order!

1 large baking potato
2 tablespoons tomato
   pizza topping sauce
1 tablespoon canned
   sweetcorn kernels
8 small slices pepperoni
1 teaspoon freshly chopped
   basil
1 tablespoon grated
   mozzarella cheese
salt and freshly ground
   black pepper

SERVES 1

Cook the potato following one of the
methods on page 11.

Once it is cooked, cut the potato in half
horizontally and place on a baking sheet which
is suitable for being placed under the grill/broiler.
Preheat the grill/broiler to high.

Place a spoonful of pizza sauce on top of each
potato half and spread out evenly, almost to
the edge of the potato. Top each half with some
sweetcorn and pepperoni and a little fresh basil.
Cover with the grated mozzarella and season
with salt and pepper.

Place the potato halves under the grill/broiler
for 3–5 minutes until the cheese has melted
and started to turn golden brown.
Serve straight away.

GOULASH

Goulash is a fiery Hungarian dish that is rich with tomatoes and (bell) peppers and flavoured with paprika. You can vary the spice level of the dish by using either sweet or spicy paprika. Both will give the dish a wonderful flavour. The recipe makes a large pan of goulash, but it freezes well so you can make and freeze in individual portions if you do not need to serve four.

4 large baking potatoes
2 tablespoons plain/
　all-purpose flour
400 g/14 oz. braising steak,
　diced
2 tablespoons olive oil
1 onion, finely chopped
1 garlic clove, finely
　chopped
1 red (bell) pepper,
　deseeded and chopped
400 ml/1¾ cups beef stock
1 teaspoon paprika
125 ml/½ cup white wine
70 g/2½ oz. tomato
　purée/paste
400 g/14 oz. can chopped
　tomatoes
150 ml/⅔ cup soured/sour
　cream, plus extra
　(optional) to serve
salt and freshly ground
　black pepper

SERVES 4

Cook the potatoes following one of the methods on page 11.

Preheat the oven to 180°C (350°F) Gas 4.

Place the flour on a plate and season well with salt and pepper. Coat the braising steak in a light dusting of the seasoned flour. Discard any excess flour. Heat 1 tablespoon of the oil in a heavy-based ovenproof pan and fry the beef for about 2–4 minutes to brown. Depending on the size of your pan, you may wish to cook in batches so that the pan is not overcrowded. Once cooked, remove the beef from the pan and blot any excess oil on the beef with paper towels. Set aside whilst you cook the onion.

Add the remaining oil to the pan with the onion and garlic and cook over a gentle heat until the onion is soft and starts to caramelize. Add a spoonful of water to the pan if they start to stick, which will loosen the onion. Once the onion has softened, add the chopped (bell) pepper to the pan and cook until soft.

Return the steak to the pan. Add the beef stock, paprika, wine, tomato purée/paste and tomatoes and season with salt and pepper. Cook in the oven for 1½–2 hours until the beef is soft and tender and the sauce is rich and thick.

Remove from the oven and stir through the soured/sour cream.

When you are ready to serve, cut the potatoes open and top each with a generous spoonful of the goulash. Top with extra soured/sour cream to serve, if you wish.

BEEF STROGANOFF

Beef stroganoff is a 1970s throwback classic – a popular dinner party dish of its time. Whilst traditionally served with rice, it is a great creamy topping for a jacket potato. If you want to serve more portions, just double the ingredients. It is good to serve with a dressed green salad on the side to cut through the rich sauce.

2 large baking potatoes
1 small onion, finely
    chopped
1 garlic clove, finely
    chopped
2 tablespoons olive oil
100 g/3½ oz. button
    mushrooms, trimmed
    and halved (if large)
150 g/5½ oz. fillet steak
2 tablespoons plain/
    all-purpose flour
3 tablespoons brandy
1 tablespoon butter
1 teaspoon wholegrain
    mustard
125 ml/½ cup hot beef stock
125 ml/½ cup soured/sour
    cream
salt and freshly ground
    black pepper

TO GARNISH
freshly chopped parsley

SERVES 2

Cook the potatoes following one of the methods on page 11.

In a heavy-based pan, cook the chopped onion and garlic in 1 tablespoon of the olive oil over a low heat. Cook slowly until the onion becomes soft and caramelized. If the onion starts to stick, add a spoonful of water to the pan. Once the onion is cooked, add the mushrooms to the pan and cook for another few minutes. Remove the pan from the heat.

Place the flour on a plate and season well with salt and pepper. Place the steak on a chopping board and bash with a meat mallet or rolling pin so that the steak is thin. Cut the steak into thin strips with a knife and coat with the seasoned flour mixture. Discard the excess flour. Heat the remaining olive oil in a frying pan/skillet until hot, then add the steak strips and pan-fry for 1–2 minutes. Depending on the size of your pan, you may wish to cook in batches so that the pan is not overcrowded. Remove the beef strips from the pan and drain on paper towels. Return to the pan with the onions and mushrooms and heat, then add the brandy to the pan and cook for a minute or two more.

Add the butter, mustard and hot stock and simmer over a low heat until the butter has melted. Stir through the soured/sour cream and heat for a further 1–2 minutes. Season with salt and pepper to your taste.

When you are ready to serve, cut the potatoes open and place on two plates. Top each with half of the beef stroganoff, garnish with parsley and serve straight away.

HAWAII POTATO

This potato is a pimped version of the classic Hawaii pizza, replacing the pizza dough with potato halves. I love the sweet and saltiness of the bacon and fruit together. The pineapple juice can be fresh, but the juice from a can of pineapple works perfectly fine, too.

1 large baking potato
2 rashers/slices smoked back bacon
1 tablespoon finely chopped onion
1 tablespoon canned or fresh pineapple pieces
1 tablespoon pineapple juice
1 tablespoon butter
2 tablespoons tomato purée/paste
2 slices Swiss cheese
salt and freshly ground black pepper

SERVES 1

Cook the potato following one of the methods on page 11.

Cut the bacon into small pieces and fry in a pan. You should not need oil as the bacon will render fat as it cooks. Add the chopped onion to the pan and fry until the bacon is crisp and the onion is soft. Add the pineapple to the pan with the pineapple juice and heat for a few minutes until the liquid has evaporated.

Cut the potato in half lengthways and preheat the grill/broiler to high.

Scoop out the potato flesh and place in a bowl with salt and pepper and the butter and mash until smooth and creamy. Return the mashed potato to the skins and place on a baking sheet. Spread a little tomato purée/paste over the top of each potato and top each with half of the bacon and pineapple mixture. Place a slice of Swiss cheese on top of each potato half and then place the baking sheet under the grill/broiler for 3–5 minutes, until the cheese has melted and starts to turn golden brown and bubble. Serve straight away.

PAPRIKA SOURED CREAM MUSHROOMS

One year I travelled to the Christmas markets at Lubeck, which is a foodie Mecca – stalls selling every delicacy you can imagine. One of my favourite treats was the paprika mushrooms, which were cooked in giant pans over open flames. Whilst they are delicious on their own, piled high on a jacket potato, this dish always transports me back to Germany.

2 baking potatoes
1 tablespoon butter
300 g/10½ oz. button
  mushrooms, halved
1 teaspoon smoked paprika,
  sweet or hot to your taste
1 tablespoon brandy
1 teaspoon freshly chopped
  parsley
1 teaspoon thyme leaves
150 ml/⅔ cup soured/
  sour cream
squeeze of lemon juice,
  to taste
freshly snipped chives
salt and freshly ground
  black pepper

SERVES 2

Cook the potatoes following the instructions on page 11.

Whilst the potatoes are cooking, melt the butter in a pan and then add the mushrooms and cook for about 5–10 minutes until softened. Add the paprika to the pan with the brandy, parsley and thyme and cook for a few minutes further. Stir in the soured/sour cream and reduce the heat to a very low setting. Season with lemon juice and salt and pepper. If the sauce splits, do not worry, just add a little more soured/sour cream and it should recover.

Cut the potatoes open and top with the mushrooms, then garnish with fresh chives. Serve straight away.

CUBAN POTATO HAM, ROAST PORK, SWISS CHEESE, PICKLES & MUSTARD DRESSING

The film 'Chef' – where chef Carl Casper sets up a food truck serving Cuban delights, which became an internet sensation – sparked a fascination with Cuban fast food for me. This Cuban-inspired potato has pork loin marinated in orange, pineapple and oregano with garlic and onion. Once pan-fried, the pork is delicious served with Swiss cheese, pickles and a mustard mayo.

2 pork loin chops
2 large baking potatoes

FOR THE MARINADE
1 garlic clove, peeled
1 small onion, finely
   chopped
200 ml/1 cup
   pineapple juice
200 ml/1 cup orange juice
1 tablespoon runny honey
1 tablespoon dried oregano
3 tablespoons olive oil,
   plus extra for frying
salt and freshly ground
   black pepper

TO SERVE
2 teaspoons Dijon mustard
2 tablespoons mayonnaise
butter (optional)
4 slices Swiss cheese
8 slices wafer-thin ham
dill pickles, sliced

SERVES 2

The day before you want to serve, prepare the marinade. Thinly slice the garlic and place in a dish that is large enough to hold the marinade and meat but that will also fit in the fridge. Add the chopped onion, pineapple and orange juices, honey, oregano and olive oil and whisk everything together. Season well with salt and pepper. Cut the pork loin chops into thin strips and place in the marinade. Stir well. Cover with clingfilm/plastic wrap and leave to marinate in the refrigerator overnight.

The following day, cook the potatoes following one of the methods on page 11.

Add a little olive oil to a frying pan/skillet, drain off the marinade (save a little to use later), through a sieve and then add the pork, onion and garlic to the hot pan. Fry for about 8–10 minutes until the pork is cooked and starts to caramelize. Season with salt and pepper, add a little of the reserved marinade to the pan and cook for a few minutes more. Keep the pork warm until you serve.

Mix the mustard into the mayonnaise and season with salt and pepper.

To serve, cut the potatoes open and top with butter if using. Place slices of Swiss cheese on top of each potato and top with the ham and hot pork mixture. Top with the mustard mayo and dill pickles and serve straight away.

NEW YORK RUBEN

I have enjoyed many a Ruben sandwich at Katz's diner in New York – the home of the famous When Harry Met Sally 'I'll have what she's having' scene. I love to flavour sauerkraut with pineapple and caraway. A Ruben sandwich is filled with pastrami – if you have a deli nearby you may be lucky enough to find home-cured pastrami – it's definitely worth it.

2 baking potatoes

FOR THE RUSSIAN
DRESSING
2 egg yolks
1 teaspoon Dijon mustard
1 tablespoon cider vinegar
200 ml/1 cup mild olive oil
1 tablespoon horseradish
1 tablespoon tomato
   ketchup
salt and freshly ground
   black pepper

FOR THE SAUERKRAUT
100 g/3½ oz. preserved
   sauerkraut
½ teaspoon caraway seeds
60 ml/¼ cup
   pineapple juice
1 tablespoon finely chopped
   pineapple flesh

TO SERVE
4 slices Swiss cheese
4 slices pastrami
butter (optional)
freshly chopped parsley,
   to garnish

SERVES 2

Cook the potatoes following the instructions on page 11.

Next, make the Russian dressing. Place the egg yolks, mustard and vinegar in a blender or food processor and blitz. Very slowly drizzle in the olive oil, blending continuously until the mayonnaise is thick. Gently fold through the horseradish and ketchup and season with salt and pepper. Store in a jar in the refrigerator until needed.

For the sauerkraut, heat the sauerkraut in a saucepan with the caraway seeds, pineapple juice and chopped pineapple for about 5 minutes. Season with salt and pepper.

To serve, cut the potatoes open and place two slices of Swiss cheese on top of each potato, adding a little butter, if you wish. Top with the hot sauerkraut, which will melt the cheese. Top with slices of pastrami and add a large spoonful of Russian dressing to each. Garnish with parsley and serve straight away.

BEEF IN BLACK BEAN SAUCE

Whilst traditionally served with rice, this popular Chinese dish works really well on top of a potato. If you prefer, you can make it with chicken in place of the beef or make this vegetarian by pan-frying additional vegetables, such as baby sweetcorn and water chestnuts.

2 large baking potatoes
1 small onion, finely sliced
1 red (bell) pepper, deseeded and sliced
1 garlic clove, finely sliced
2.5-cm/1-inch piece of ginger, peeled and thinly sliced
1 tablespoon sesame or olive oil
200 g/7 oz. fillet steak
2 spring onions/scallions, trimmed and sliced
75 g/2½ oz. mangetout/snow peas
100 g/3½ oz. black bean sauce
butter, to serve (optional)

SERVES 2

Bake the potatoes following one of the methods on page 11.

Heat the oil in a wok or frying pan/skillet until hot, add the sliced onion and (bell) pepper, garlic and ginger and fry for about 3–5 minutes until the onion and (bell) pepper are soft. Take care to stir all the time so that the garlic does not burn.

Place the steak on a chopping board and bash with a rolling pin, then cut into thin strips. Add the steak to the hot pan and fry for a few minutes until cooked. Toss in the spring onions/scallions and mangetout/snow peas and fry for a couple more minutes, then add the black bean sauce and heat until the sauce is piping hot.

Cut the potatoes open, add butter, if you wish, and then top with the beef in black bean sauce. Serve straight away.

MAPLE-ROASTED BEETROOT WITH TZATZIKI

Beetroot has a wonderful earthy flavour and when roasted takes on a delicious sweetness. The beets in this recipe are roasted with balsamic and maple syrup for a sweet and sour flavour. You can use a combination of yellow and red beetroot if you want this dish to look extra pretty.

2 large baking potatoes

**FOR THE
MAPLE ROASTED
BEETROOT/BEETS**
2 whole raw beetroot/beets,
   washed
½ tablespoon olive oil
½ tablespoon balsamic
   vinegar
½ tablespoon maple syrup
salt and freshly ground
   black pepper

FOR THE TZATZIKI
200 g/1 cup Greek yogurt
½ garlic clove
½ teaspoon salt
¼ cucumber, trimmed
1 teaspoon dried oregano
½ teaspoon mint sauce
   or freshly chopped mint

TO GARNISH
1 tablespoon freshly
   chopped mint

SERVES 2

Cook the potatoes following one of the methods on page 11.

Preheat the oven to 180°C (350°F) Gas 4.

Cut the beetroot/beets into quarters. There is no need to peel them although you can, if you wish. Place the eight beetroot/beet quarters in a roasting pan and drizzle with the olive oil, balsamic vinegar and maple syrup. Season with salt and pepper and roast in the oven for 30–40 minutes until the beetroot/beet feels soft when you insert a sharp knife into the centre. Remove from the oven and leave to cool.

Whilst the beetroot/beets are cooking, prepare the tzatziki. Place the yogurt in a bowl. Crush the garlic with the salt using the back of a knife so that it makes a paste, and add this to the yogurt.

On a coarse grater, grate the cucumber, including the peel but do not grate the middle watery part of the cucumber. Place the grated cucumber in a clean kitchen towel and squeeze out the water. Alternatively, you can do this by squeezing using clean hands. Remove as much water as possible then add the grated cucumber to the yogurt. Add the oregano and mint and mix everything together. Season with salt and pepper, cover and store in the refrigerator.

When you are ready to serve, cut open the potatoes and top each with a generous amount of tzatziki, then top with the roasted beetroot/beets. Sprinkle with freshly chopped mint and serve straight away. You can add butter to your potato before topping with the tzatziki, if you wish.

HAGGIS & WHISKY SAUCE

Haggis – the national dish of Scotland – is somewhat of an acquired taste and I would be the first to admit that the thought of it can be a little off-putting. But you have to trust me that it does taste delicious and paired with a whisky sauce, it makes a rich and tasty supper. Haggis is traditionally served with Neaps and Tatties (turnips and potatoes) which makes a jacket potato the perfect accompaniment for haggis. You can serve with a side of turnips as well if you want to be super traditional.

4 large baking potatoes
400 g/14 oz. haggis

**FOR THE
WHISKY SAUCE**
1 large onion,
    finely chopped
1 tablespoon butter
3 tablespoons whisky
125 ml/½ cup vegetable
    stock
1 teaspoon wholegrain
    mustard
125 ml/½ cup double/
    heavy cream
salt and freshly ground
    pepper

**FOR THE
BACON LATTICE**
8 rashers streaky bacon
24 fresh chives

SERVES 4

Cook the potatoes following one of the methods on page 11.

Cook the haggis following the packet instructions and keep warm until you are ready to serve.

For the sauce, in a frying pan/skillet, cook the chopped onion in the butter until it is soft and starts to caramelize. If the onion starts to stick or burn, add a little water to the pan. When the onion is soft, pour the whisky into the pan and cook for a few minutes. Add the stock and cook down until the stock has reduced by half. Add the mustard and cream and simmer over a gentle heat until the sauce thickens. Season with salt and pepper and keep warm.

Preheat the grill/broiler to high.

To make the bacon lattices, cut the bacon into thin strips about 10 cm/4 inches in length so that you have eight for each lattice. Weave the bacon strips and chives in the way shown in the photograph using the under/over method on a sheet of foil on a baking sheet to make four lattices. Grill/broil for 3–5 minutes, turning halfway through cooking, until the bacon is cooked.

To serve, cut the potatoes open and top each with a slices of the haggis. Pour over the whisky sauce and top each with a bacon lattice. Serve straight away.

SAAG PANEER

4 baking potatoes

FOR THE RUB
1 tablespoon olive oil
1 teaspoon curry powder
   or garam masala

FOR THE SAAG PANEER
400 g/14 oz. paneer
1 tablespoon olive oil
2 tablespoons ghee
1 large onion,
   finely chopped
1 garlic clove,
   finely chopped
2.5-cm/1-inch piece of
   fresh ginger, peeled
   and finely chopped
1 red chilli/chile, deseeded
   and finely chopped
2–3 curry leaves
2 teaspoons garam masala
1 teaspoon ground cumin
1 teaspoon black
   onion seeds
1 cinnamon stick
500 ml/17 oz. passata/
   strained tomatoes
1 tablespoon clear honey
100 g/3½ oz. baby spinach,
   washed
100 ml/scant ½ cup
   double/heavy cream

TO SERVE
freshly chopped
   coriander/cilantro
chopped pistachios

SERVES 4

Paneer cheese is a wonderful Indian ingredient. With a rich tomato and spinach sauce, this is perfect on jacket potatoes when it's cold outside. The list of ingredients may look long, but they just get added to the pan to simmer at the same time, so it is honestly an easy dish.

Before cooking the potatoes, mix together the olive oil and curry powder/garam masala for the rub and place in a small clean plastic bag. One at a time, place the potatoes in the bag and rub them with the spiced oil. Place on a baking sheet and cook following the oven method on page 11.

For the saag paneer, cut the paneer into cubes. Add the olive oil to a pan and fry the paneer on all sides until lightly crisp and golden. Remove the cheese and drain any excess oil on paper towels. Wipe the pan dry.

Add 1 tablespoon of the ghee to the pan and add the onion, garlic, ginger and chilli/chile and fry over a gentle heat until the onion is soft. Add the second tablespoon of ghee to the pan and add the curry leaves, garam masala, cumin, black onion seeds and cinnamon stick to the pan and fry over a gentle heat to warm the spices for a few minutes. Add the passata/strained tomatoes to the pan with 100 ml/⅓ cup plus 1 tablespoon water and the honey and simmer the sauce for about 20 minutes until it has thickened. Add the spinach to the pan, which will cook in the heat of the sauce in a few minutes. Next, add in the paneer and the cream and stir through so that the cream is warmed.

When you are ready to serve, cut the jacket potatoes open and top each with a portion of the saag paneer. Garnish with coriander/cilantro and chopped pistachios and serve straight away.

SATAY CHICKEN

Satay chicken is one of my favourite dishes with its rich coconut-peanut sauce. The sauce is quick to prepare and if you use ready-cooked chicken, you can make a delicious potato topping in no time at all. Add spring onions/scallions, chopped peanuts and chilli/chile for a colourful garnish. Soy sauce often contains gluten so if you want to make this gluten-free make sure that you use a gluten-free brand – tamari soy sauce is usually gluten-free.

2 baking potatoes
250 ml/1 cup plus
   1 tablespoon
   coconut cream
1 tablespoon soy sauce
1 tablespoon soft
   dark brown sugar
2 tablespoons crunchy
   peanut butter
freshly squeezed juice
   of 1 lime
1–2 tablespoons fish sauce
2 ready-cooked chicken
   breast, skins removed

TO GARNISH
1 spring onion/scallion,
   trimmed
2 tablespoons peanuts
1 tablespoon
   freshly chopped
   coriander/cilantro
1 red chilli/chile,
   finely sliced
lime wedges (optional)

SERVES 2

Cook the potatoes following one of the methods on page 11.

In a saucepan, heat the coconut cream, soy sauce, brown sugar, peanut butter and lime juice together over a gentle heat, whisking so that the sugar and peanut butter dissolve. Add the fish sauce to your taste – I like a lot, but it can be strong so it is best to add a spoonful at a time. Once the sauce is hot, chop the chicken into small pieces and add to the sauce. Heat until the chicken is hot.

Whilst the chicken is cooking, prepare the garnishes. Slice the spring onion/scallion into very thin slices and place in a bowl of cold water. This will cause the spring onion/scallion to curl. Finely chop the peanuts.

Cut the cooked potatoes open and top each with half of the satay chicken. Drain the spring onion/scallion from the water and use to garnish each potato, together with chopped coriander/cilantro, peanuts and red chilli/chile slices. Serve with lime wedges.

DHAL & RAITA

Making dhal could not be simpler – just simmer a large pot with ingredients on the stovetop and then finish it off with a hot spiced ghee. Steven Wallis of Masterchef fame taught me everything I know about dhal – he used to make it for us when we were competing on the show.

4 baking potatoes

FOR THE DHAL
250 g/9 oz. red split lentils
1 small onion,
    finely chopped
1 teaspoon ground turmeric
2 teaspoons curry powder
2.5-cm/1-inch piece of
    fresh ginger, peeled
    and finely chopped
1 red chilli/chile, whole
400 g/14 oz. can chopped
    tomatoes
1 teaspoon fenugreek
    powder
1 cinnamon stick
salt and freshly ground
    black pepper

FOR THE TARKA
2 tablespoons ghee
1 tablespoon black
    onion seeds
2 garlic cloves, finely sliced
1 tablespoon curry leaves

FOR THE RAITA
¼ cucumber, finely chopped
250 ml/1 cup plus 1
    tablespoon natural yogurt
a pinch of salt
2 teaspoons cumin seeds

TO GARNISH
fresh coriander/cilantro

SERVES 4

Cook the potatoes following one of the methods on page 11.

For the dhal, place the red lentils and chopped onion in a large heavy based saucepan with 1.25 litres/5 cups of water and place over a gentle heat. Add the turmeric, curry powder, ginger, red chilli/chile, tomatoes, fenugreek and cinnamon stick and simmer for about 45–60 minutes until the lentils are soft and have absorbed most of the water. If the water evaporates before the lentils are really soft, add a little more water to the pan. Season with salt and pepper. The lentils should have thickened to a soup-like texture.

To finish the dhal, prepare the tarka by melting the ghee in a frying pan/skillet. Add the onion seeds, garlic and curry leaves and cook for a few minutes until the garlic is lightly golden brown and the onion seeds start to pop. Pour into the lentils all in one go but save a tablespoon to drizzle over the potatoes as garnish. The dhal will sizzle as you do this. Cook the dhal for a further 5 minutes so that the flavours of the ghee infuse into the lentils.

To prepare the raita, remove the seeds from the cucumber using a teaspoon to scrape them out and finely chop the cucumber. Add to the yogurt with salt and the cumin seeds and stir together.

To serve, cut the potatoes open and place each in a dish. Spoon over the dhal and top with a large spoonful of the raita. Garnish with coriander/cilantro and serve straight away. The dhal will keep for up to 3 days in the refrigerator or can be frozen.

DANISH AGURKESALAT WITH SALMON

Agurkesalat is a Danish speciality of pickled cucumber which is perfect to serve with cold meats and fish. This recipe was given to me by my lovely Danish friend Deborah – it's her family recipe. The pickling liquor is sweet with sugar and sour from the vinegar and has a heady fragrance of dill. It makes a great potato topping with salmon.

2 large baking potatoes
125 ml/½ cup white wine
   vinegar
100 g/½ cup white sugar
½ cucumber
2 tablespoons freshly
   chopped dill
2 poached/ready-cooked
   cold salmon fillets
salt and freshly ground
   black pepper

TO SERVE
2 tablespoons crème fraîche
1 lemon, cut into wedges

SERVES 2

Cook the potatoes following one of the methods on page 11.

Put the vinegar, sugar and 125 ml/½ cup of water in a bowl and whisk until the sugar has dissolved. Cut the cucumber into very thin slices using a mandolin. If you do not have a mandolin, cut into thin slices using a sharp knife. Add to the pickling liquid and stir in the dill. Season with salt and pepper. Cover and put in the refrigerator for at least 30 minutes or longer if you are able to.

When you are ready to serve, drain the cucumber salad. In a bowl, break up the salmon fillets into large chunks, then add the cucumber slices and stir through. Cut the potatoes open, divide the cucumber salad between the potatoes and top each with a spoonful of crème fraîche. Season with a little more salt and pepper and serve straight away with lemon wedges.

SCANDI MEATBALLS
WITH LINGONBERRY JAM

I may be biased but my brother Gareth makes the best meatballs ever! Although he usually makes them with pork, on my last visit to his home in Brooklyn he made this delicious lamb version stuffed with tangy feta cheese. Served with warmed lingonberry jam, they go perfectly on top of a potato for a complete meal-in-one. Make the meatballs small so that you can fit plenty of them on top of the potato.

4 large baking potatoes
500 g/18 oz. lean
   minced/ground lamb
1 egg
80 g/3 oz. Panko
   breadcrumbs
100 g/³/₄ cup feta cheese,
   chopped into small cubes
1–2 tablespoons oil
250 g/9 oz. lingonberry jam
   or redcurrant jelly
salt and freshly ground
   black pepper

SERVES 4

Cook the potatoes following one of the methods on page 11.

Whilst the potatoes are cooking, prepare the meatballs. Place the lamb into a large mixing bowl and season well with salt and pepper. Whisk the egg and add to the lamb along with the pankobread crumbs. Mix everything together with your clean hands so that all of the egg and breadcrumbs are incorporated into the meat.

Take a small portion of the lamb mixture and press out on the palm of your hand. Place a small piece of feta cheese in the middle and then bring the lamb mixture up over the cheese to form small balls. Make about 25–30 small meatballs, although you can make larger ones if you prefer.

In a frying pan/skillet, heat the oil until hot and then add the meatballs to the pan. Cook for 10–15 minutes until the outside of each meatball is golden brown. Test if they are done by removing one of the meatballs and cutting open to check that the meat is no longer pink.

In a saucepan, heat the lingonberry jam or redcurrant jelly over a gentle heat so that it becomes viscous. When you are ready to serve, cut the potatoes open and top each with a portion of meatballs. Pour over the hot sauce, season with a little more salt and pepper and serve.

SPANISH PATATAS BRAVAS

Patatas Bravas is a fiery Spanish tapas dish with crisp potatoes. In this recipe, to get the crispy equivalent of the traditional fried potatoes, once the jacket potatoes are cooked, you cut them in half and place them, skin side down, on an oiled tray so that they become crispy.

2 large baking potatoes
olive oil, for drizzling
freshly chopped parsley,
   to garnish

**FOR THE SPICY
TOMATO SAUCE**
1 small onion,
   finely chopped
3 garlic cloves,
   finely chopped
1 red chilli/chile, deseeded
   and finely chopped
1 tablespoon olive oil
400 ml/14 oz. passata/
   strained tomatoes
1 teaspoon paprika
1 teaspoon honey
salt and freshly ground
   black pepper

FOR THE GARLIC AIOLI
2 garlic cloves, peeled
½ teaspoon salt
2 egg yolks
1 teaspoon Dijon mustard
250 ml/1 cup plus
   1 tablespoon light
   olive oil
a squeeze of lemon juice

SERVES 2

Bake the potatoes in the oven following the method on page 11. Once the potatoes are cooked, remove them from the oven, but leave the oven on at 180°C (350°F) Gas 4.

When the potatoes are just cool enough to handle, cut them in half lengthways. Pour a little olive oil onto a baking sheet and place into the oven until it is hot. Place the potatoes, cut side down, on the oiled baking sheet and bake for about 15 minutes until the potatoes have crisped and are golden. Keep warm until you are ready to serve (you can prepare the tomato sauce and aioli in advance, if you wish, and serve as soon as the potatoes are cooked).

For the spicy tomato sauce, place the chopped onion, garlic and chilli/chile in a large frying pan/skillet with the olive oil and fry over a gentle heat until the onion is soft and translucent. Add the passata, paprika and honey to the pan and season with salt and pepper. Simmer for about 10–15 minutes until the sauce has thickened. Keep warm or reheat to serve.

For the aioli, crush the garlic with a little salt to a paste. Place the garlic in a food processor with the egg yolks and mustard and blend together. Very slowly pour in the olive oil whilst still pulsing so that the sauce emulsifies into a thick mayonnaise. Add a squeeze of lemon juice and season with salt and pepper to taste. Cover and store in the refrigerator until you are ready to serve.

Place your crispy potatoes on serving plates and top with the tomato sauce and garlic aioli. Garnish with some freshly chopped parsley and serve straight away.

BAKED & BEYOND

JACKET POTATO SOUFFLÉ

Soufflés are usually a cook's nightmare as they can sink if you don't serve them quick enough. These soufflés are more stable as they are made with mashed potatoes, and so although they don't puff up as much as a traditional lighter soufflé, they won't sink as quickly. By adding whisked egg white to the potato, this makes a very light and airy dish. To change the flavour of your soufflé, you can add some grated cheese with the mash, if you wish.

2 large baking potatoes
2 tablespoons butter
1 teaspoon wholegrain mustard
2 eggs, separated
salt and freshly ground black pepper

SERVES 2

Cook the potatoes following one of the methods on page 11. Remove from the oven and when cool enough to handle, slice the tops off the potatoes. Scoop out the potato flesh, leaving enough potato in the skins so that they hold their shape. Place the scooped-out potato in a bowl with the butter and mash until smooth. Beat in the mustard and egg yolks and season well with salt and pepper.

Preheat the oven to 180°C (350°F) Gas 4.

Place the potatoes on a baking sheet.

In a separate clean, dry bowl, whisk the egg whites to stiff peaks and then fold gently into the potato mixture with a spatula. Spoon the soufflé mixture into the potato shells. Bake for about 30 minutes until the soufflés are golden on top. Serve straight away.

LOADED JACKET SKINS

These loaded potatoes are a perfect party food but are equally good in an individual portion. You can flavour the filling with anything you choose really. I have used bacon, spring onion/scallion and Cheddar cheese, but other ideas are sun-dried tomatoes, chopped olives and feta or pesto and cheese.

1 large baking potato
80 g/3 oz. pancetta cubes
1 tablespoon butter
40 g/scant ½ cup Cheddar cheese, grated
1 spring onion/scallion, trimmed and finely chopped
salt and freshly ground black pepper

SERVES 1

Cook the potato following one of the methods on page 11.

Place the pancetta in a dry frying pan/skillet and fry for about 5 minutes until the pancetta is crisp and slightly golden brown. You do not need to add any oil when cooking as the pancetta will render fat as it cooks. Stir the pancetta regularly in the pan so that it does not burn. Leave to cool slightly.

When the potato is cool enough to handle, carefully cut into quarters and scoop away more of the potato, leaving the skins with enough potato on so that they hold their quarter shape. Place the scooped-out potato in a bowl with the butter, season with salt and pepper and mash well. Add the pancetta pieces, most of the cheese, reserving a little of the cheese to sprinkle on top of the wedges, and the spring onion/scallion and stir everything together.

Preheat the grill/broiler to high.

Place spoonfuls of the potato mixture back into each wedge and place on a baking sheet. Sprinkle with the reserved cheese and place under the grill/broiler for about 5 minutes until the cheese starts to turn golden brown. Serve straight away.

GIANT HASSELBACK BAKED POTATOES

Hasselback potatoes are always a great dish to serve because they have that wow factor when you take them out of the oven, with the thin scored slices crisping as you roast them and giving the potatoes almost a hedgehog effect when they are done. These giant versions are even more fun as you can stuff between the slices using any fillings you like really – I have used mozzarella and tomato and sage and bacon, but the possibilities for this dish are endless – garlic butter, pesto and sun-dried tomatoes, blue cheese and walnut. Be as creative as you wish!

4 large baking potatoes
1 tablespoon olive oil,
    plus extra for drizzling
salt and freshly ground
    black pepper

FOR FILLING OPTION 1
1 ball mozzarella cheese
1 large tomato

FOR FILLING OPTION 2
2 slices smoked back bacon
handful of sage leaves

SERVES 4

Preheat the oven to 200°C (400°F) Gas 6.

To prepare the potatoes, place chopsticks or two wooden spoon handles along the long sides of one of the potatoes. On a chopping board, carefully cut very thin slices in the potato cutting only as far as the wooden handles/chopsticks so that the bottom of the potato remains intact. Repeat with all the remaining potatoes. Rub all of the potatoes with olive oil and sprinkle with freshly ground sea salt.

Place the potatoes in a roasting pan and bake in the oven for 45 minutes.

Remove the potatoes from the oven. Depending on which filling you are using, cut the mozzarella and tomato or bacon and sage leaves into thin slices and place alternating pieces of each between the slices in the potatoes. Depending on how thin you have cut your slices, you may find it easiest to insert filling every second slice rather than in between each slice. Drizzle with a little more olive oil and season with salt and pepper, then return to the oven and bake for a further 15 minutes. Serve straight away.

LASAGNE LAYERED BAKED POTATO

Lasagne is a great prepare-ahead dish. This version replaces the pasta with layers of fluffy jacket potato, making it a hybrid of lasagne and moussaka.

4 large baking potatoes

FOR THE MEAT FILLING
1 onion, finely chopped
2 garlic cloves, crushed
1–2 tablespoons olive oil
400 g/14 oz. lean
    minced/ground beef
1 carrot, peeled and
    coarsely grated
400 g/14 oz. can chopped
    tomatoes
70 g/2½ oz. tomato
    purée/paste
250 ml/1 cup plus
    1 tablespoon red wine
500 ml/2 cups plus
    2 tablespoons beef stock

FOR THE CHEESE SAUCE
2 tablespoons butter
2 tablespoons flour
200 ml/1 cup milk
120 g/1⅓ cups grated
    Cheddar, plus extra
    for sprinkling
pinch of grated nutmeg
salt and freshly ground
    black pepper pepper

6 x chef's rings that are
    about the diameter
    of your potatoes

6 x pieces of foil, larger
    than the chef's rings

SERVES 6

Prepare the meat filling the day before you want to serve. In a large pan, fry the onion and garlic in the olive oil until the onion has softened and started to turn light golden brown. Add the beef to the pan and fry until the meat has browned. Add all the remaining ingredients and simmer for 1 hour until the sauce has thickened and most of the liquid has evaporated. Leave to cool, then store in the refrigerator overnight.

Cook the potatoes following one of the methods on page 11.

Prepare the cheese sauce. Heat the butter in a pan over a gentle heat until melted, then add the flour and whisk to incorporate into the butter. Cook for a few minutes, taking care that the mixture does not burn. Whisk in the milk, a little at a time. Add the cheese to the sauce and whisk over a gentle heat until the cheese has melted and the sauce has thickened. Season with salt and pepper and a little nutmeg. Cool.

Preheat the oven to 180°C (350°F) Gas 4.

Cut the cooked potatoes into round discs. Grease the chef's rings and a baking sheet with a little butter. Fold one piece of foil up around the edges of each chef's ring. Place on a baking sheet. Carefully place a large disc of potato in the bottom of each ring. The potato should fill the ring, so if it does not do this, cut up additional pieces of potato and press into the gaps. Next, place a spoonful of the meat on top of the potato and cover with a spoonful of cheese sauce. Place another layer of potato on top and repeat with the meat and cheese layers. Sprinkle over a little extra grated cheese.

Bake in the oven for 15–20 minutes until the top is golden brown. Remove from the oven and leave to cool for a few minutes. Remove the foil, place each ring on a serving plate then lift up the ring. Serve with salad.

FISH PIE

This recipe makes the perfect use of a jacket potato. Potato skins hollowed and filled with fish in a cheesy white sauce with the potato piped into a classic pie topping. I like my fish pie to have a cheesy sauce, but you can omit the cheese and just use the white sauce, if you prefer.

4 large baking potatoes
300 g/10½ oz. fresh fish pieces such as salmon, haddock, cod and raw peeled shrimp/prawns
100 g/¾ cup frozen peas
2 tablespoons milk
2 tablespoons butter
1 tablespoon freshly chopped parsley
salt and freshly ground black pepper

FOR THE CHEESE SAUCE
2 tablespoons butter
2 tablespoons plain/ all-purpose flour
400 ml/2 cups milk
120 g/1⅓ cups grated Cheddar cheese, plus extra for sprinkling
1 teaspoon wholegrain mustard

piping/pastry bag with large star nozzle/tip

SERVES 4

Cook the potatoes following one of the methods on page 11. When the potatoes are cool enough to handle, cut off the tops of the potatoes and scoop out the flesh into a mixing bowl. Leave enough potato around the edge of the skins so that they hold their shape and will be a stable bowl to contain the fish pie filling. Add the milk and butter to the potato and mash until smooth. Season with salt and pepper. Spoon the mashed potato into the piping bag and reserve until you are ready to top the potatoes.

Whilst the potatoes are cooking, prepare the cheese sauce. Heat the butter in a saucepan over a gentle heat until melted, then add the flour and whisk to incorporate into the butter. Cook for a few minutes over the heat, taking care that the flour mixture does not burn. Slowly whisk the milk in a little at a time so that lumps do not form. Add the grated cheese to the white sauce with the mustard and whisk over a gentle heat until the cheese has melted and the sauce has thickened. Season with salt and pepper.

Preheat the oven to 180°C (350°F) Gas 4.

Add the fish and peas to the cheese sauce and spoon into the potato skins. Pipe the potato on top of the potatoes to cover the fish pie filling. If you do not have a piping bag, spoon the potato on top and make soft peaks or patterns with a fork. Sprinkle with extra grated cheese. Place on a greased baking sheet and bake in the preheated oven for 20–25 minutes until the tops of the potatoes are golden brown. Serve straight away with chopped parsley to garnish.

MINI DEEP-FRIED BAKED POTATOES

Technically speaking, as these are new potatoes, you could argue that they do not deserve a place in this book – however, I love serving them as canapés, so I am going to sneak this one in and hope you will forgive me. These little potatoes are deep-fried in a tempura beer batter to give them a crispy coating. At German Christmas markets crispy potato rosti are served with apple sauce on the side so that's my recommendation as a dip for these too as potatoes and apple are a match made in heaven.

750 g/26 oz. new potatoes
150 g/1 cup plus
    2 tablespoons
    self-raising/rising flour
100 g/³/₄ cup cornflour
1 teaspoon baking powder
200 ml/1 cup light beer
200 ml/1 cup ice cold
    sparkling water
1 litre/4 cups frying oil
    such as vegetable oil
salt and freshly ground
    black pepper
apple sauce, to serve

SERVES 8 AS A SNACK

Preheat the oven to 200°C (400°F) Gas 6.

Place the potatoes in the roasting pan and bake for 30–40 minutes until the potatoes are soft and a knife cuts in easily when you place it in the centre. The actual cooking time will depend on the size of your potatoes so check then regularly after 25 minutes.

In a bowl, whisk together the flour and cornflour with the baking powder, beer and sparkling water to a smooth batter. Pass through a fine mesh sieve to remove any lumps. Season with salt and pepper.

Pour the frying oil into a deep pan and heat to 180°C/350°F. If you do not have a thermometer to test if the oil is ready add a little of the batter to the oil, if it starts to sizzle immediately the oil is hot enough to cook.

Place the cooked potatoes in the batter and toss so that they are well coated. Then remove with a spoon and place quickly in the hot oil. Deep-fry the potatoes until they are golden brown, then remove with a slotted spoon and drain on paper towels. It is best to cook in batches so that you do not overfill the pan.

Season the warm potatoes with plenty of salt and pepper and serve with apple sauce for dipping.

BURGER SLIDERS

If you are looking for the ultimate feast, then this is the jacket potato
for you. The potato is used in place of a burger bun and sandwiches
a delicious pork and apple pattie with crispy onions and apple sauce.

4 baking potatoes

**FOR THE
BURGER PATTIES**
½ onion, finely chopped
1 tablespoon butter
2 sage leaves,
   finely chopped
1 apple, grated
500 g/18 oz. minced/
   ground pork
1 egg
50 g/2 oz. panko
   breadcrumbs
1 tablespoon olive oil

**FOR THE
CRISPY ONIONS**
1 onion, sliced into rings
500 ml/2½ cups milk
   or enough to cover
   the onions
1 tablespoon Worcestershire
   sauce, plus extra
   to sprinkle
100 g/¾ cup plain/
   all-purpose flour
1 litre/quart frying oil,
   uch as rapeseed
salt and freshly ground
   black pepper

TO ASSEMBLE
1 Little Gem/Bibb lettuce
apple sauce
mayonnaise

SERVES 4

Bake the potatoes following one of the methods on page 11.

For the patties, put the onion in a frying pan/skillet with the
butter and the sage and fry for a few minutes until the onion
is translucent and the sage is crisp. Add the apple and cook
for a few minutes. Remove from the heat and cool.

For the crispy onions, put the onion rings in a bowl with the
milk, making sure that the onions are completely covered,
add the Worcestershire sauce and leave to soak for 30 minutes.
Place the flour on a plate and season well with salt and pepper.
Drain the milk from the onions and discard it. Place the onions
on a plate and sprinkle with a drizzle of extra Worcestershire
sauce. Toss the onions in the flour mixture. Set aside.

Place the pork in a mixing bowl. Beat the egg and add to the
pork with the breadcrumbs and the cooled apple and onion
mixture. Season with salt and pepper and mix together with
your hands. Divide the mixture into four and form into patties.

Add a tablespoon of oil to a clean frying pan/skillet, add the
patties and fry for 8–10 minutes turning occasionally until
golden brown on both sides. Keep warm.

Just before you are ready to serve, heat the oil in a pan until
hot. Test if it is hot enough by adding a small piece of onion
to the pan and if it sizzles and turns golden brown it is ready.
Add the onions to the pan and fry until they are golden brown.
Remove from the oil using a slotted spoon and drain on paper
towels. Season with a little salt and pepper.

To serve, cut the potatoes in half horizontally and place one
half on each plate. Add lettuce leaves, a pattie, apple sauce and
mayonnaise to each then add crispy onions. Place the second
potato half on top and secure in place with a wooden skewer.

CHICKEN & LEEK POT PIES

Topped with crisp puff pastry these little pies are a meal in themselves.

4 large baking potatoes
300 g/10½ oz. ready-made
   puff pastry
1 egg
flour, for dusting
salt and freshly ground
   black pepper

FOR THE CHICKEN
250 ml/1 cup plus 1
   tablespoon white wine
1 carrot, roughly chopped
1 onion, roughly chopped
2 bay leaves
2 skinless chicken breasts,
   cut into 3-cm/1¼-inch
   pieces

FOR THE FILLING
1 large leek, trimmed and
   sliced
50 g/3½ tablespoons butter,
   plus extra for mashing
1 tablespoon cornflour
1 heaped tablespoon
   wholegrain mustard
125 ml/½ cup double/heavy
   cream

FOR THE WINE SAUCE
500 ml/2 cups plus 2
   tablespoons of the
   reserved chicken stock
200 ml/1 cup double/heavy
   cream
1 teaspoon wholegrain
   mustard
1 tablespoon cornflour
1 tablespoon butter

SERVES 4

Cook the potatoes following one of the methods on page 11.

Pour the wine into a pan with 1 litre/4 cups of water and add the carrot, onion and bay leaves. Bring the liquid to the boil. Add the chicken to the pan and simmer for a few minutes, then remove from the heat and leave for 20 minutes. Check that the chicken is cooked, then strain the poaching liquid and reserve to use later.

In a large frying pan/skillet, fry the leek in the butter, season and cook until soft. Add the cornflour to the pan and stir then add the chicken and mustard. Add the cream and 100 ml/⅓ cup of the reserved chicken stock simmer for a few minutes until the sauce starts to thicken. Remove from the heat and let cool.

Cut a small hole in the top of each cooled potato. Scoop out the flesh but leave a layer of potato around the edge of the skin. Place the scooped-out potato into a bowl, mash with butter and season to taste. Spoon the chicken mixture into the cavity of each potato so that it is a little higher than the top of the potato.

Preheat the oven to 180°C (350°F) Gas 4.

On a flour-dusted surface, roll out the pastry to 5 mm/¼ inch thickness and 1–2 cm/½–¾ inch larger than the opening on the top of each potato. Beat the egg and brush a thin layer of egg over one side of the pastry. Taking each in turn, with the egg side down, place the pastry over the potato and smooth down. Use a fork to make crimped edges on the pastry. Brush the top of the pastry with egg and cut a small hole in the top of each pie.

Place the potatoes on a baking sheet and bake in the oven for 25–30 minutes until the pastry is golden brown.

For the sauce, put the reserved chicken stock in a pan with any leftover filling and simmer until the liquid has reduced by half. Add the cream to the pan with the mustard. Rub the cornflour into the butter and add to the pan, then simmer until the sauce thickens. Strain and serve warm with the pies and mash.

BAKED EGG FLORENTINE

Traditionally, eggs are baked in small dishes in the oven with a filling beneath. Here the dish is replaced with the potato shell, which makes an ideal cooking vessel plus it makes the dish more substantial.

1 large baking potato
100 g/3½ oz. spinach
2 tablespoons butter
½ small onion,
    finely chopped
80 ml/⅓ cup double/
    heavy cream
pinch of grated nutmeg
1 egg
1 tablespoon freshly grated
    Parmesan cheese
salt and freshly ground
    black pepper

SERVES 1

Bake the potato following one of the methods on page 11. Leave to cool.

Cook the spinach in a pan of salted water for 3 minutes until it is soft, then drain immediately and blanch in cold water. When the spinach is cold, drain and place in a clean kitchen towel, then squeeze out as much water as you can.

Preheat the oven to 180°C (350°F) Gas 4.

Place the spinach on a chopping board and roughly chop.

Heat 1 tablespoon of the butter in a frying pan/skillet and add the chopped onion. Cook until the onion is very soft and starting to caramelize which will take about 3–5 minutes. Add the chopped spinach to the pan and cook for a few minutes to remove any excess moisture. Add the cream to the pan and season with the nutmeg, salt and pepper. Cook for a few minutes until the cream has thickened and reduced.

Carefully cut away the top of the potato, making sure that you only cut a circle in the middle and that you leave a good edge, as this will be the sides of your baking dish. Scoop out most of the potato, but make sure that you leave about a 2 cm/¾ inch edge of potato all the way round. Mash the potato with the remaining tablespoon of butter and season then return to the bottom of the potato. The potato should be about half full.

Spoon the creamed spinach into the cavity on top of the mash so that it is almost full, but it is important to leave room for the egg. Place the potato on a baking sheet. Make a small dip in the centre of the spinach mixture and break in the egg. Sprinkle over the Parmesan and a little salt and pepper. Transfer the sheet to the oven. Bake in the oven for 10–15 minutes until the egg is just set on top. Serve straight away.

INDEX

ACKNOWLEDGMENTS

With all my thanks to the wonderful team at RPS as always for publishing such a beautiful book, particularly to Julia Charles my fabulous friend for commissioning the book and allowing me to indulge my comfort food cravings. Special thanks to Toni Kay for the wonderful design and Miriam Catley for the patient editing. Steve and Lucy as always you have worked wonders – transforming the humble spud into elegant photographs – you are the best photo team a girl could wish for. To the wonderful BARAKURA ENGLISH GARDEN in Chino, Japan and particularly the Yamada Family where I spent many hours writing this book – thank you for the wonderful Japanese hospitality and recipe inspiration – your garden is the most magical and special place and I was honoured by my time with you x

To my Mum and Dad, Gareth, Amy, Hunter and Bo and all my friends and family who ate potatoes in the scorching heat of summer when all you really wanted was salad – thank you all for always being there, forks in hand, to help out as my taste testers – you are the best x